I'M JUST SAYING

A Guide to Maintaining Civil Discourse
in an Increasingly Divided World

MILAN KORDESTANI

Health Communications, Inc.
Boca Raton, Florida
www.hcibooks.com

Library of Congress Cataloging-in-Publication Data
is available through the Library of Congress

© 2023 Milan Kordestani

ISBN-13: 97807573-2450-5 (Paperback)
ISBN-10: 0-7573-2450-9 (Paperback)
ISBN-13: 978-07573-2451-2 (ePub)
ISBN-10: 0-7573-2451-7 (ePub)

Publisher: Health Communications, Inc.
          301 Crawford Blvd., Suite 200
          Boca Raton, FL 33432-1653

Cover design by Olivia Maria Chevallier
Interior design and formatting by Larissa Hise Henoch

Contents

~

vii   Foreword

1   Introduction
Let's Talk

Part I: The Foundations

23   Chapter One
Reflection

53   Chapter Two
Intention

73   Chapter Three
Tone

93   Chapter Four
Trust

iii

Contents

Part II: In Practice

121   Chapter Five
Active Listening

141   Chapter Six
Being Attentive

161   Chapter Seven
Maintaining Focus

Contents

~

Part III: Overcoming Challenges

185   Chapter Eight
Seeking Common Ground

207   Chapter Nine
Expecting Conflict in Perspectives

227   Chapter Ten
Avoiding Poor Discourse

247   Epilogue
Civil Discourse Going Forward

257   Endnotes and Recommended Readings

260   Acknowledgments

262   About the Author

Foreword

~

Milan Kordestani's *I'm Just Saying* is a touching *cri de coeur* of a young man who wants to take what the poet Robert Frost would have called the "road less traveled." His effort is daring and touching, lofty in its goals, articulate in its plan of action. His passion is less for the world of capital accumulation and more for the intellectual, emotional, and symbolic capital requisite to maintain the civility needed for sustaining a democratic society. In recent years, scholars have been warning of a crisis of democracy, of a "democratic deficit," of a frightening increase in the number of authoritarian countries, and ultimately of threats to even established democracies like the US and many parts of Europe. I'm Just Saying is a noble effort to apply tools of technology to the much-needed task of preserving democracy.

Discourse is the very foundation of democracy. It is based on informed dialogue and a mind open for change; its nemesis is a closed mind moored to the dictates of ideology. It requires empathy, patience, and humility for the other; its enemy is the self-righteous rancor and hubris of a solipsist. In our benighted days, when many of the crypto capitalists and digital billionaires are hatching dreams of creating colonies in space or adding new billions to their wealth without regard for the cost to society or the environment, Milan has set himself the Herculean but commendable task of saving and promoting the indispensable pillar of democracy. The enormous complexity of the task has not dissuaded him from making a remarkable assay; in that sense, *I'm Just Saying* is an assay—whence comes the more commonly known word essay—describing his commendable journey on this infinitely complex path.

I have known Milan since he was a young boy precociously concerned about the perils to our ecosystem. He turned parts of the backyard of his family home into an organic farm. He planned every step, studied every trope, and took rightful pride in his products. As he planned his college career, he again avoided the accruements of affluence to which many of his peers aspired. He chose his college based only on one criterion: an institution where he could best nurture and intellectually empower his passion for nature. After college, instead of wallowing in comforts of extreme affluence, he began studying and marshaling his unique experiences, his connections and talents, and his affluence to his socially conscious passion. Here, too, he is taking the road less traveled.

Three of my colleagues at Stanford, Rob Reich, Mehran Sahami, and Jeremy M. Weinstein, all involved in one way or the other with teaching computer science and the ethics and politics of the digital age have published a fascinating and frightening book entitled *System Error: Where Big Tech Went Wrong and How We Can Reboot.* More than anything it is a lament, a siren song, about the worrisome

preoccupation of the tech-savvy, entrepreneurially minded generation of brilliant young students keen on only developing applications
that are the shortest routes to fabulous wealth. The moral, ethical,
and social consequences of their innovation, the authors say, is
often of little concern to them. Even noble efforts to democratize
the digital age, they suggest, is often demonized by big tech companies. As the Romantics like Mary Shelley showed us more than a
hundred fifty years ago, technological development bereft of moral
compunction and diligent attention to the quarks of our individual
characters begets only a Frankenstein.

I'm Just Saying is not just a word of warning about the emerging
Frankenstein of intolerance, but it is also an earnest, tech-savvy,
entrepreneurially minded, morally conscientious assay at fashioning
a democratic, tolerant, self-aware, and self-critical citizenry—the
very foundation of an enduring democracy. It might seem like a
Romantic dream, but it is a Romanticism with the best of intentions and informed about the perils to democracy in this pivotal
moment. What Milan is "just saying" might indeed be what we just
need to heed.

                              —**Abbas Milani,** Director of the Iranian Studies
                                       Program at Stanford University

Introduction:
Let's Talk

My first business was dealing turtles.

Kind of. My dad bought me Sheldon (whose name I have changed to respect his privacy) when I was thirteen years old. Wanting a turtle was a natural byproduct of my fascination with ecosystems—you know, a typical thirteen-year-old's interest! There was something alluring to me about the self-sustaining sphere of an ecosystem. It exemplified the cycle of life and death—the inescapable wheel we're all a part of. And Sheldon needed that ecosystem to thrive. He needed all those moving parts, those aspects of the ecosystem that spoke and responded to one another. I realized that Sheldon, despite becoming more of a best friend, could also help me make money. I could get a lot from breeding turtles. That's when I took the plunge into the world of entrepreneurship.

Turtle husbandry, in many ways, was a conversation. I had to be aware of and adjust the environment—did they have enough light? How was the temperature? Was the water filter functioning? Intricate actions on my part, though meaningless to me, had a huge impact on the result. Incubating the eggs properly, and rotating them at the right time, could affect how the turtles turned out. To some extent, I had control over what kind of turtle was produced, though there was also so much beyond my reach.

If breeding the turtles was a conversation, then the topics were albino red-eared sliders, albino map turtles, and albino yellow-bellied turtles. With carefulness and planning, I could create shells in various morphs—mohawk shapes and bright colors. These turtles had bright red eyes. And people paid a lot for them.

Then, as a turtle seller, I also had to *have* conversations—not with my turtles (though I still did), but with the people I was selling to. I'd had conversations before, of course, but now they carried more weight. Now, my words meant the difference between closing a deal and losing out on a great opportunity. I had to refine my conversation like it was a sleek, brightly colored shell. And I couldn't always shape the outcomes in the moment. Sometimes successful conversation meant thinking in the long term. Sometimes I had to walk on eggshells—not literally, of course.

Those turtles taught me so much about words.

A LITTLE BIT ABOUT ME

Who am I to know what's best for civil discourse? It's a valid question, and I'll say this: I'm just proposing solutions—which is at the heart of civil discourse—and inviting discussion from those who either agree or disagree. I'm just one human. I hadn't even heard the term *civil discourse* until I realized why I valued anonymous publishing around the age of twenty. However, I did understand something at a younger age, and that was the concept of cultivating happiness through having great conversations with others. I realized that my emotions could deeply affect others around me, and if I exuded positivity, it would make others around me more likely to do the same. I also learned the same is true for negativity.

I was fortunate enough to be born into wealth and perhaps even more fortunate to have a close guide in my life, who I'll call Jay. Jay once told me that because my family was wealthy, how I treated the people who could do nothing for me would be the only way I'd gain the respect of people who would actually care about me in my life. That's because people would see showing kindness to the person who is least likely to do something for you as a sign of true respect because it would be kindness for kindness' sake, not for any other motive. I learned that it doesn't matter your background, wealth level, upbringing, opinions, or anything else—every person is a human being and deserves to be reckoned with on a human-to-human level.

I grew up in Silicon Valley—a place surrounded by wealth and business success. There, people were so wealthy that they were too afraid to spend their money or help the next generation build projects. Many people hoarded what they had and only thought about how they could make more for themselves without truly giving back. Seeing this demotivated me. Plenty of people there were reluctant to spend their vast sums of money or allow for new building projects for the next generation. I couldn't help but wonder why these people, who were much more fortunate than so many others, were not enticed to give back and make the world a better place.

As I was growing up, my parents constantly told me that I would struggle to succeed because I didn't view success as life or death. I had lived a life of privilege, and I internalized my parents' doubts, but doing so paralyzed me. For years, that attitude kept me lonely and isolated from others. I thought that my "chase" would never align with that of my friends or peers. I imagine there are many individuals from successful parents who have had a similar experience.

Though painful, isolation and loneliness are fundamental aspects of the human condition that we can all understand. When you start to feel isolated from certain social groups—let's say the wealthy spend more time with the wealthy and less time seeing homelessness—the surrounding echo chamber can get louder. You can get further out of touch with the reality other people from different backgrounds face. Isolation is the disconnection. It can feel cold and troublesome and can be experienced even if you're surrounded by people. It can also happen if you feel like you're not going to achieve the level of success you constantly see around you because the (often unrealistic) expectation can be placed on you to achieve what appears to be normal within the echo chamber.

The more you're disconnected from people who are different from yourself, the more you intentionally isolate yourself to avoid awkwardness. This awkwardness can lead to a downward spiral that negatively affects civil discourse. The more isolated you feel, the more isolated you act. You end up being less likely to make a positive impact in your quick interactions throughout life. You're more likely to be bitter, less civil, and more combative rather than collaborative. You may cope by becoming defensive, which is a dangerous thing to feel when trying to engage in civil discourse.

If you ever feel isolated like I did and you're looking to repair that sense of connection with others, that's something *I'm Just Saying* is setting out to do. It is possible for us to default to civil discourse rather than the opposite. We've spent years living the lie that technology is going to bring us closer. The fact is that it hasn't. It's siloed us and stopped us from being able to cultivate people skills that are fundamental to help make our world a better, more understanding place. Technology has made it difficult for us to engage in the necessary civil discourse that this world needs.

Still, I was determined to ensure that my isolation was productive. I wanted to be able to thrive in other areas of my life. I found companionship in animals—like turtles and chickens. I found a profound sense of solace in researching ecosystems, writing, and diving into tech. However, before I even turned sixteen, I had always thought of myself as the "other." This sense made me more defensive, more isolated, and less likely to engage in essential and open conversations with my fellow humans. I found it extremely difficult to make friends, find common ground, and communicate at all. I had no idea how to say what it was I was thinking clearly, or how to get my ideas out into the world via respectful, productive speech. I was terrified of the rejection that may have come with expressing myself.

One problem I had with communication was that my first language was Farsi, my second was Spanish, and my third was English. My mother has prioritized language, culture, and the pursuit of understanding people my entire life. She deeply believed in ensuring great communication and learning about others because that made life more joyful. But it was difficult for me being in English-speaking schools. Not being entirely fluent in English made connecting with English speakers a struggle. My family and I had spent years traveling back and forth to Iran, so making friends and conducting discourse really stretched my abilities.

Due to the language barrier, I've always had to be very intentional with my words. It's probably why I've always been able to communicate via writing more effectively—because I know it gives me a chance to write something, think, and edit—so I can say what is true to me to the best of my ability. It's also why I strive to be as clear and accommodating as possible to others because I want them to understand my intentions the best they can. For me, excellent communication is at the forefront of my life and in everything I do. I'm careful not to offend people, and I always try to remember that my intentions may be misunderstood. Of course, there has to be a willingness, trust, and openness from the speaker *and* listener to ensure messages are appropriately sent and received. However, I know that the only thing I have control over is how I conduct myself.

I always try to be conscious and deliberate in how I communicate, though I don't get it right all the time—who can? I embrace that, though. Knowing that I will inevitably make mistakes helps me remember that I can keep improving my communication. If you have this same attitude, it's likely the same will be true for you. Slowly and carefully picking words has been fundamental to my past and present, and I wouldn't have it any other way. This ensures more conflict-free interactions, where everyone starts from the same foundation of faith and trust.

There was a time in life when I was tired of explaining, defending myself, and feeling like the "other"—the kid that struggled to speak clearly in his third language. I'm sure a lot of people feel this way—maybe even you have. But to continue through life assuming that other people are out to get you or are so different from you that you can't relate to them is not a way you want to live your life. If we put up barriers between ourselves and others, understanding will only decrease. The more that happens on the individual level, the more it will happen on a societal level. So it's up to us to stop this communication breakdown in favor of something greater.

All these experiences led to the quote that I try to take into consideration as much as possible: "How you treat the person who can do nothing for you is how people will perceive you." When I allowed the nutrients of this quote to truly spread throughout my body, I realized that my goal did not center on money but on having a profound and positive impact on as many people throughout my life as I could. When I appealed to this higher purpose, I found an attitude focused on giving back to humanity rather than seeing what I could extract from it. My life—including how I spent my time, how I interacted with others, and how I understood my purpose on this planet—completely changed for the better.

But why civil discourse? Well, it became intensely important to me because I started to understand that every micro-interaction I had formed the macro of my entire lifetime. Even if other people treated me differently, it was up to me to have faith that I could find common ground with everyone I interacted with. I learned that I should trust myself and my intentions in guiding any conversation toward having a positive outcome.

The final component in civil discourse is the faith that people in your life will understand your intentions when they see you pushing for civil discourse over debate or reactionary discourse. When I decided to become intentionally positive in every human interaction to the best of my ability, I had to learn that people who knew me from before I applied these principles would question my behavior. What I found was that in explaining my behavioral change I usually inspired others to seek change as well. Someone who may have been more combative before started responding more positively. I started seeing the benefits in how I took ownership of how I used to act. Furthermore, I had to practice faith and patience for those who used to know me as more reactionary than civil.

THE SHOCKING LACK
OF DISCOURSE IN COLLEGE

In the fall of 2017, at the age of seventeen, I got accepted to Colorado College. I was so excited to experience vastly diverse thinkers, open-minded discussions, a collective zest for learning, and abounding creativity throughout the next four years. That is what all of us are promised upon entering college—the joy of being able to share fresh ideas with our peers, right? Curiosity buzzed inside me. What new discourses would form the next chapter in the book of my life? What sort of person was I going to become, faced with the unique and invigorating challenges of college?

To my surprise and great displeasure, college did not turn out to be the intellectual utopia I had envisioned. I had expected that the seminars that dozens of students and I attended would allow us to debate the great philosophers like Kant and Plato, discuss various psychology theories from Freud and Jung, and apply their ethics to modern challenges. I thought we were going to discuss everything from what we thought about climate change to politics, covering all sorts of issues considered contentious in our world. I even prepared to lounge in frat house living rooms and dorms to discuss start-up ideas and our individual experiences, all to inspire fresh thinking and self-reflection.

Unfortunately, reality sliced in and proved to be a sharp contrast to my—perhaps naive—expectations. Instead of sounding boards, I felt myself stuck on a linear track. I wasn't in an open field, discussing ideas and having intriguing discussions with people from different walks of life. Now, I was trapped inside the confines of an echo chamber. What I experienced flummoxed me: students were reluctant to disagree on readings or videos. It was rare to find students who were willing to voice a political, economic, or social opinion that directly disagreed with their professors in graded or shared assignments. All around me, people were either terrified of not conforming, or we were in a space where conformity was all the norm. I was starting to get suspicious that this wasn't unique to Colorado College and probably extended to the wider world.

My high school friends had similar experiences. Common complaints with some of them sounded something like "No one wants to voice an opinion," and "Everyone focuses on competition rather than collaboration." As the years progressed, I realized that my suspicions were confirmed: my college experience was not atypical—the free exchange of ideas was lacking from other colleges, too.

Most campuses, it seems, struggle to support diversity of thought. Students are either like-minded or quiet about their "different" views. The problem is that many students mask how they really feel because of fears, some of them imagined, some of them very real, including potential repercussions like social isolation, canceling, or doxing (the malicious online publication of private information to encourage harassment). Faculty, which increasingly consisted of adjunct professors and graduate students who feared professional consequences, also felt the need to self-censor. Over the years, I have met more and more people who have had similar experiences to mine.

I later found out that the lack of civil discourse I experienced at Colorado College was not unique to my college, or even post-secondary institutions, for that matter. Political discourse in the United States, and abroad, has devolved into literal shouting matches—political point scoring, people giving others a "piece of their mind," and other unproductive modes of dialogue. This happens all over the place, even during what you'd hope would be otherwise civilly conducted political debates or congressional hearings.

To compound issues, in order to stay relevant in our modern world—one where we're bombarded with a barrage of digital update after update—old school media relies on provocation to stay relevant. Online spaces are only receiving more and more angry levels of feedback, so readers—with anger eliciting the most feedback—just feed into increasingly extreme views. Comment sections for online news now need to be moderated thanks to this aggressive behavior. Specific Reddit threads, and even entire platforms like Parler, have become associated with disruptive, conspiracy-laden, and insurrectionist social discourse. It has become nearly impossible to find consistently civil discourse within the American public sphere, no matter the medium.

Public distrust of media, antagonism on digital platforms, doxing, and threatening behavior have only become amplified since we started spending more and more time online, privy to algorithmic systems that show us things we're more likely to engage with. Things like widespread propaganda and conspiracy campaigns have spread like a disease. The once-calm, meaningful, and productive conversations focused on shared truths and understanding have pretty much completely unraveled. Civil discourse, it appears, is broken.

But is it beyond repair?

AIMING TO FIX THE ISSUE: THE DOE

In my sophomore year of college, I dreamt up an idea that would change the course of my life forever and, I hoped, help change the world forever. My aim was to build a company that would play a part in solving one of the greatest problems of our time: the decline of civil discourse. I was privileged enough to have the means and resources needed to try to fix it. So I gathered a team, and in 2019, we launched an anonymous publishing company, *The Doe*.

The Doe was a forum where online contributors could publish their perspectives and spark civil discourse on controversial, critical, and even dangerous topics. Our objective was to provide a safe and unbiased platform for marginalized voices and viewpoints, where users could publish articles anonymously to the public. Writers would go through our processes to verify identities and the authen-ticity of shared narratives—all without revealing their information to the public. This provided our readers and writers with a whole new media experience.

I was excited by what we'd built, but I was especially floored by the response. In its second year alone, *The Doe* amassed a global readership of nearly 1 million, along with 500,000 followers and 30,000 subscribers. It helped prove that the world was hungry for a new online publication—one that supported not only anonymity but diversity in people, viewpoints, and narratives.

In removing the opportunity to attack an author person-ally—thus enforcing a degree of civility—*The Doe* created a space primar-ily focused on narrative content and ideas, discouraging personal attacks. Writers from all walks of life and political realms shared sto-ries from their lives they otherwise never would have shared. Writers described the experience as cathartic, and our fol-lowers described the content as echo chamber-breaking. Members of minority groups could share narratives that would have led to ostracism within their communities, or even death threats from oppressive groups. Our publication's anonymity allowed writers to comfortably and safely publish insights for readers to absorb. It let the public practice civil discourse surrounding seldom-discussed topics or viewpoints on regularly discussed topics that were pushed down. In short, *The Doe* encouraged unique perspectives to flourish. A key to civil discourse, after all, is perspective. Even if you can't relate to someone else's experience, knowing and understanding it (with context) can help create a connection that doesn't just help build knowledge but bridges, too.

In our early days of ideating and founding *The Doe*, it was paramount that I invested my time and energy into building a new publication "for the people." At the time of *The Doe's* inception, there was nowhere for the non-influential person with a unique and compelling story to share their perspective without having to face the externalities of bylining, or putting their names on a vulnerable piece that could lead to ramifications in the wider world. That "for the people" mindset was exemplified in our stringent verification of our authors' articles. It was evident in our promise to be as unbiased as possible in presenting their stories. Sometimes, we needed to turn away beautifully written and compelling stories because an author refused to comply with our verification process. While we wanted to be able to publish as much as we could, it was up to us to ensure that our users could trust that each anonymous author was telling the truth. Without trust, discourse breaks down—the antithesis of everything at *The Doe*.

The process at *The Doe* involved collecting personal information for every contributor—including their political affiliation, age bracket, and career—then publishing monthly stats for each demographic category on social media. This way, the public could hold us accountable if we were becoming too focused on one group's views.

If we had a few months of liberal-heavy content, we boosted our network of dozens of conservative thought leaders, asking for more input from alternative voices in order to balance the discourse as much as we could. Our goal was to provide a safe publication for all voices to be equally expressed to ensure civil discourse could once again became the dominant paradigm in the American public consciousness.

Of course, not every story successfully resonated with readers. Sometimes we published a piece knowing that our audience would hate it and that we could end up losing thousands of followers. That was the level of controversy we often dealt with. We accepted this challenge as a part of helping rebuild civil discourse. Just because some people weren't ready to hear an opposing perspective didn't mean we shouldn't publish it. In fact, we believed that controversy was often *necessary* in creating a safe space for communication.

It is only by hearing opposing perspectives that we can truly strengthen our own opinions or have ours significantly challenged to the point that we might—*wait for it*—change our minds. Opposition helps us to either clarify our own thinking or shift our thoughts, opinions, and actions entirely.

In short, civil discourse doesn't always mean agreeing or feeling comfortable. The same could be said about exercise. Muscle doesn't grow without resistance. Similarly, uncomfortable conversations challenge us, and it is only through challenge that we become the most resilient. If we forgo civil discourse in favor of a shouting match to insult the person we disagree with, all we do is awaken someone to their defensiveness. Ultimately, this just reinforces a speaker's original opinion at best and adds more muscle strength to their convictions at worst. Therefore, if you walk away from a conversation proud that you were able to give the other person "a piece of your mind," they might just be walking away thinking the same thing. Everybody loses.

In true civil discourse you must ask yourself the point of delivering your message and what emotion conveys it best. For this reason, we believed that it was our responsibility at *The Doe* to create tools and offer resources that informed readers rather than shocked, attacked, or turned them defensive.

The publication was just one of many tools I've created in pursuit of revitalizing civil discourse. I'm also committed to the research and documentation of how exactly we arrived where we are today. I will continue to explore possible solutions to help navigate civil discourse in the future. There were plenty of failures in our attempts to ignite civil discourse through *The Doe*, but each of these was part of the challenge—an important milestone along the learning curve. If I were constantly met with agreeableness, I wouldn't have been able to refine the publication.

As I describe in later chapters, some topics produced heated online discussions that required significant moderation and editorial consideration. There are plenty of examples of our readers failing to keep discussions civil. Many users brought their own, usually emotionally charged biases to the table and fought until their "opponent" conceded. What that usually meant, though, was that the other person walked away angry and probably in search of another outlet for complaints. These types of combative discourse were the exact types of discussion that we at *The Doe* aimed to reduce in society. Alternatively, some readers simply lost faith in the media and saw our publication—especially with anonymous contributors—as just another branch of the disastrous, toxic mediascape.

It was hard work, but I didn't look at these problems and throw up my hands in exasperation. When readers were irate, I chose to reflect on the controversy.

Civil discourse isn't entirely gone or unattainable, though it sometimes feels that way. On the contrary, civil discourse has always existed somewhere, and glimpses of it do exist today. We saw it over and over again on *The Doe*. We just need to know where to look, as there are many simple and easily executable tools out there that can help rebuild that discourse. We just need to work together to make the necessary changes in our day-to-day interactions. The more we change ourselves and our conduct, the better the example we'll set and the better the world we will live in.

REBUILDING CIVIL DISCOURSE

One pathway to rebuilding civil discourse lies in identifying and overcoming biases, but we require more to solve the problems that confront us. Over the years, community members have become afraid to speak up because of potentially hostile environments where differing opinions are disregarded, mocked, and shouted down before they even have a chance to be fleshed out. By overcoming biases—be it through a closer and more honest examination of ourselves, deeper self-knowledge, an understanding of the patterns of thoughts and behaviors we experience, or any other method—we can undo these mental blocks and reignite a passion for honest, genuine, and well-intentioned discourse.

The primary objective of a mutually beneficial, productive discussion is not to debate your side until you are the last one standing but to bring an open mind and awareness to understand where alternative opinions come from. We have all had different life experiences that bring us to our conclusions, and we are all malleable upon the discovery of new information. In neuroscience, there's a term called *neuroplasticity*, in which the brain is able to develop and change throughout life. It means we are all able to shift our thinking should the discourse be put forward in the best possible way. Understanding and not misrepresenting someone else's viewpoint is the key to rebuilding our world and deepening human-to-human empathy. This empathy transcends political borders and reaches beyond the liberal-conservative paradigm by deconstructing echo chambers in favor of a more open and honest discourse.

Discourse can break down at any time and in any field—during any topic of conversation—in the same way that physical objects tilt toward entropy over time. For example, arguments over who *should* have won a sports championship have led to fistfights. Perhaps you're having a casual, everyday conversation with your friend about movies. The next thing you know, you're shouting about whether or not it's immoral to support "problematic" filmmakers like Woody Allen or Roman Polanski.

Of course the stakes are even higher with politics, which causes many people to double down on their biases or their win-at-all-costs mentality. But uncivil discourse can take hold of conversations over even the most mundane and insignificant topics.

THE PURPOSE OF THIS BOOK

I've written *I'm Just Saying* not only to help you practice civil discourse but also to help you find greater balance in your daily life. In the following chapters, I will guide you through real-life stories of people who overcame obstacles and found success by engaging genuinely with themselves and others. I will also include stories from my own life. I will discuss the pushback I received when building start-ups, which helped me reflect on my own values and purpose in fostering civil discourse. I will share other observations that I hope will provide insight into the essential nature of civil discourse—including, believe it or not, a time I fell off a horse—and the steps needed to engage in it.

In essence, *I'm Just Saying* is a rumination on—and celebration of—civil discourse. You will discover what it can do, what it can't do, and how we as individuals in a society can work to rebuild it. But before we get into the nuts and bolts of reconstructing civil discourse, I'd like to give you a brief history of discourse and its deep-rooted connection with the human experience.

I'll start with some hard-hitting honesty. I'm not going to pretend to be a miracle worker—reading this book will not solve the issue of civil discourse overnight. The topic at hand is intricate, complex, and far-reaching in scope. It involves a myriad of influences and societal mechanisms that have been thousands of years in the making. Fixing civil discourse overnight would be like demolishing a home and rebuilding it in a minute. That said, civil discourse is not rocket science. You do not need a particular degree or in-depth knowledge to understand and learn from the stories outlined in *I'm Just Saying*. I'd like to think of this book as a seed that will help us grow from the soil of misunderstanding into the light of civil discourse. As you turn these pages, just remember that civil discourse is just the start of a kinder, more connected, and more open-minded global society.

To me, and I'm sure if you're reading this, it's clear that the rules of engagement for civil discourse have been broken. Even if we could eliminate the punitive pieces of the puzzle, we're still caught in a kind of deadlock, with all sides incentivized to remain oblivious to—and often actively dismissive of—others. We're simultaneously limited in what we're "allowed" to say while actively contributing to unproductive discourse online and off. In many ways, we are molded by societal forces beyond our direct control.

Deep down, most of us should recognize the resulting group-think as a farce. The human experience is too varied and complex to boil discourse down to black or white, good or bad, just or unjust. Although it's a human impulse to take shortcuts, simplify, and rein-force already-held opinions, it's essential that we avoid categorizing things so easily, which will prevent us from falling into the many logical fallacies so many of us are privy to. In reality, the things that defy categorization can often teach us the most. That's why I've written *I'm Just Saying*. I want to explore the ever-dwindling vitality of civil discourse in today's world while also drawing insight from historical examples. In the following chapters, you will encounter a thorough exploration of the human experience of discourse using real-world stories and case studies.

Though I will navigate you through these stories and provide my insight as an entrepreneur, I'm not going to beat you over the head with my opinions. Think of me as the narrator—or maybe tour guide—on this journey through the rise and fall of civil discourse. More importantly, I will provide you—the reader—with tools and strategies for entering, navigating, and engaging in civil conversa-tions. I'll do this by simulating civil discourse itself in the form of questions and answers that will appear at various points in each chapter. In doing so, I hope that we might climb out of this seem-ingly bottomless pit where we often find ourselves when it comes to having impactful, genuine, and productive conversations with others. Ultimately, I want to instill in you an excitement to restore civil discourse and, with time, bring about a revolution of ideas built on respect and compassion for one another.

Curious? So am I. Let's dive in.

Part I
The Foundations

Chapter One
Reflection

During COVID, I shared a tweet without giving it as much thought as I should have. I wrote:

> If you don't come out of this quarantine with:
> —a new skill
> —a new side hustle
> —more knowledge
>
> You never lacked time; you lacked discipline!

This tweet got a lot of attention, some good, some bad. Some even called me out for "Hustle Porn"—the glorification of the grind, pushed mostly by entrepreneurs or entrepreneurial types. Hustle culture mantras imply that you're only worth something if you're working hard every hour of the day and suffering for your work. It can be toxic, admittedly, when people demonstrate how hard they're working, throwing it on social media, and lauding it over others as a badge of pride as if it's shameful to rest. I'd say that was a fair criticism of my tweet's tone, especially when so many people have to labor tirelessly and can still barely afford to keep the lights on.

Rather quickly, I realized that this tweet was not a great way to think and that posting it demonstrated that I did not fully understand my position of privilege. Telling everyone that they needed to be smarter, more skillful, and more productive didn't take a wide range of experiences into consideration—especially because of what so many were going through as the result of the COVID-19 pandemic.

Many responders (rightly) accused me of:

- Not being supportive of those worried about their own and their families' health.
- Being insensitive to those who didn't have the means—in terms of time, health, or money—to start a new venture.
- Not considering those who had other, more pressing matters—like family obligations—that they had to deal with.
- Forgetting the essential workers who never had a chance to quarantine in the first place.
- Lacking compassion for others.
- Making light of the COVID precautions by treating them like free time.

The responses to my tweet highlighted the purpose of discourse. My critics spotted errors in what I said and called on me to look at the situation—which most people experienced differently than I did—with a little more nuance.

I could have gotten defensive, lashed out, or deleted it and pretended like it didn't happen, but I wanted to use my viral tweet as a learning experience. I looked inward. I thought about my mental blocks and the fact that they existed in the first place. While it really isn't fun to get piled on by thousands of strangers (I don't recommend it), I wasn't reflecting so I could make myself look better. I reflected because I genuinely wanted to avoid hurting others in the future and stop myself from spreading a message that was harmful in so many ways.

In the previous chapter, we briefly touched on self-reflection. I had to self-reflect to learn properly from the tweet that left a sour taste in many people's mouths. To show how this can be done, we are going to take a deeper dive into reflection more generally and how reflection affects civil discourse.

Civil discourse is a multiperson interaction. When we prepare for discourse, we focus on our arguments and whether or not we will be presenting convincing points. We think about what we need to do to change minds and influence others. When you're about to engage in a dialogue with someone, it is important to consider how they will think and react to different ideas or situations. Many people assume that civil discourse is only about adjusting to external forces in this way, but it's not. It must instead start with the act of self-reflection, ideally on the part of all parties involved. In other words, people often think that to practice discourse, they simply need to focus on the qualities and attributes of the other people involved, when they should actually begin by looking inward to learn more about themselves.

When you start driving, you should always check the road for other cars—but your first priority is to fasten your seatbelt. Similarly, looking inward is the best possible way to attain civil discourse. As we discussed previously, to look at yourself and understand yourself is generally the best way to improve communication. When you know what makes you tick or react, or what might pull a less-than-ideal reaction out of you, you can best calm yourself down. Furthermore, if you're in a discussion and you feel the rising tide of anger in your chest, reflect. If you know yourself well, you might know to take a deep breath to compose yourself before carrying on. You will have achieved the necessary self-knowledge that you need to engage in civil discourse.

It's not always easy to take note of your shortcomings. Even if you tend to be a self-aware person, you may not always like what you see. Your ego can form a protective barrier around you, making you less likely to understand your, let's say, *less positive* attributes and behaviors. When this happens, you could be tempted to hide or simply ignore aspects of yourself that are unseemly, embarrassing, or (what you or society deems) unfit for public consumption. While this might help you get a good night's sleep, it won't help you grow as a person, live genuinely, or participate in civil discourse. Gaining ease with self-reflection allows you to maintain perspective as you engage in discourse and avoid assumptions.

Let's examine the activity and purpose of self-reflection, especially as it relates to civil discourse. To do this, I thought I'd focus on some of my own experiences in business, along with some Western and Eastern philosophy so that we can talk about ideas of bias and rightness. Let's explore why self-reflection is necessary for open conversations, why it is often overlooked, and how you can practice self-reflection in your everyday life.

Self-Reflection
QUESTIONS AND ANSWERS

Q: How will self-reflection make me better at civil discourse?

A: Self-reflection allows us to become aware of our biases, which affect how we listen during discourse, how we treat others, and where we may have blocks or are prone to misjudgment. Self-reflection can help us think about our flaws and accept the fact that we are not always right—no one is. Through self-reflection, we take the time to take an honest account of ourselves, leading to more open and nonconfrontational conversations with others.

Q: How do I know if I'm engaging in honest self-reflection?

A: Honest self-reflection is true self-reflection. If you hear yourself saying things like "I knew I was right," or "So-and-so has no idea what they're talking about," you may be reflecting, but you're not reflecting honestly. Honest reflection is when you can take a step back and look at yourself as a product of different life experiences. When you bypass the inner, ego-driven voice, a voice of conscience can speak up. Far from the overly critical voice of the ego, this voice tends to let us know when we are too harsh, get something wrong, or need to deepen our empathy. You may not always know if your self-reflection is honest, but listen to the reflection. Is it a calm and composed voice you're interacting with or a cyclone of thoughts?

Q: How will self-reflection make me better at handling uncivil discourse?

A: Self-reflection improves civil discourse by pushing you toward reason. You've likely met people who seem to have virtually no self-awareness. They haven't taken the time to reflect upon their beliefs or their way of being, so if you attempt to enter a discourse that challenges some aspect of their ideas, they may answer with confusion or even hostility. Fortunately, self-reflection gives you the tools to act with a greater sense of reason and cooperation in civil discourse. This way, you're far less likely to feel the compulsion to fight fire with fire.

Additionally, self-reflection is a great way to rid yourself of harmful beliefs or traits that could make it harder to handle uncivil discourse. You won't completely change who you are overnight, but taking note of your shortcomings is the first step toward self-improvement. So, if you tend to get very angry when people challenge your beliefs, self-reflection can help you identify this trait and overcome it with time.

BIASES AND DISCOURSE

Self-reflection comes in many forms: contemplation, questioning of the self, or focus exercises to better understand your values, abilities, weaknesses, biases, and more. Those who tend to be highly critical of themselves take self-reflection to an extreme, twisting it into something more disorderly. Sometimes it becomes self-criticism to the point that it functions as more of a hindrance than a help. In this example, your ego might give you an extremely difficult time—leading to negative thoughts and feelings. This is less reflective and far more damaging. It's important, therefore, to decide whether you're being too critical, not critical enough, or inauthentically reflective. However, for the vast majority of us, self-reflection is a practice that must be cultivated. Self-reflection is about fostering a degree of objectivity. With objectivity, we can recognize our biases and prevent those biases from getting in the way of civil discourse.

For better or worse, we see the world through a singular lens that often causes us to fall victim to certain biases. I've seen a number of entrepreneurs who built successful businesses and attributed all of their achievements to their own ingenuity. These people tend to lack the self-reflection and objectivity to see that their accomplishments likely would not have been possible without the assistance of various people and institutions external to themselves. It's all too easy to see failures in our lives as purely or predominantly due to outside (external) forces, and successes in our lives as purely or predominantly due to inside (internal) forces. Therefore, we must know that credit must be given and shared. Apple's success wasn't exclusively Steve Jobs's, nor was Microsoft exclusively Bill Gates's. Santa has thousands of little helpers who allow him to achieve the impossible. It takes a team of people (or elves) and a huge network for us to accomplish anything. Even the experience of going to the market and buying food is a result of someone farming it, building vehicles to transport it, shipping it, and putting it on display in the store for sale. There's a lot more going on than purely internal self-will.

So how can one become more objective if we are inherently subjective creatures? I'd like to begin this part of the discussion by saying that complete objectivity is impossible. Instead, it is the target at which self-reflection should aim—to recognize where our objectivity falters and thus where we have predispositions and weaknesses.

To better illustrate this point, let's look at the example of the *Allegory of the Cave* first introduced in the writings of Plato. It will help us to see how our biases and subjective perspectives cause us to misread situations and miscast our discursive partners. For those who are unfamiliar with Plato's *Allegory of the Cave,* it goes something like this:

Prisoners are chained against the wall of a cave, unable to turn their heads in any direction. Above them, but out of sight, a fire is lit, where puppeteers walk and go about their daily puppetry business. These people cast shadows against the cave's far wall, which is the only thing that the prisoners below can see. Thus, the prisoners mistake appearance for reality. They think the things they see on the wall (the shadows) are real. They know nothing of the true causes of the shadows. When the prisoners are released, they turn their heads and see the actual objects. Furthermore, they leave the cave and experience the sun and the real objects of our world.

Plato equates this revelation to the discovery of "the Good," which he sees as something perpetually out of reach but necessary for the understanding of all other things. The pursuit of objectivity is much like Plato's pursuit of "the Good." We all have aspects of the cave in our lives—responsibilities, roles, and relationships that serve as chains to limit our perception, creating biases that we do not even realize exist. While we may never free ourselves entirely from the cave, we can come closer to the concept of objectivity by accepting the limitations of our subjectivity. Rather than assuming that we are right—that we know everything that we know without any need for doubt—we must accept that we are not faultless. Humans are flawed, without exception (sorry, Beyoncé). By accepting our limitations, we can practice self-reflection to enhance civil discourse. We must acknowledge that there are truths outside our perceptions from our personal spot in the cave.

But more importantly, Plato's story teaches us a valuable lesson about reflecting on our own position while engaging in civil discourse. Like the prisoners chained to the wall of Plato's Cave, we cannot see everything around us. We can easily make assumptions based on the selective evidence gathered from our own position. Sometimes, our instinct is to shape the truth in line with our own biases. We can learn from this example by questioning them and thinking about what we might not be seeing that affects our decisions.

BIAS
QUESTIONS AND ANSWERS

Q: Where do biases come from?

A: Our biases come from a variety of circumstances, many outside our control. We are taught how to live *in* our culture *by* that culture (a dizzying feedback loop). With that reality comes certain paradigms that may hold us back in life as we diversify our experiences. We may develop preferences based on interactions or experiences we have had, lending too much weight to specific situations and letting that cloud our perspectives. No matter where biases come from, we internalize them. We can also choose to stop internalizing them and improve our discourse.

You can also develop an implicit bias, one that exists in your mind, even if you're not aware of it. This is often the most nefarious kind of bias as it can make civil discourse much more difficult. You may have grown up hearing that a certain group of people were inherently superior to others. Even if you don't explicitly support this point of view, you may have an implicit (subconscious) bias in favor of this group nonetheless. If you remain unaware of this implicit bias, you will act in the world in a way that's unjust or unfair. It's essential, therefore, to uncover your biases as much as possible, and honest self-reflection will help get you there.

Q: How do I determine what biases I have?

A: The best way to identify your biases is to evaluate your feelings in relation to other people and things. During self-reflection, think about a particular group of people. What emotions arise in you when you think about them? Anger? Contempt? Jealousy? Happiness? Admiration? Indifference? Based on how you implicitly react, you can start to see how you may be biased in your way of thinking. You can do this at both the micro-level (i.e., your feelings toward someone in your friend group) and the macro-level (your feelings toward a particular political movement or group).

Q: Am I a bad person if I'm biased?

A: Not at all—everyone has biases! From our upbringing to our education to our occupation, our positions in the world shape our views and inevitably cause some biases. Many of our biases come from lessons learned or stories told that we have internalized, just as society teaches us to behave in certain ways. Having biases doesn't make you bad—it makes you normal! But we can always change our minds about our biases. We can learn to think about them in more reasonable ways. The challenge is bringing them into our awareness. Once we are aware, we can start to unpack. We can manage our biases and prevent them from shaping our discourse or behavior.

Q: Can't it be good to have biases?

A: It can be good to have preferences. But having biases means giving too much weight to certain ideas, more than they deserve. You let the bias do the thinking for you. Biases are the foundations of prejudice and mistrust, and thus have no place in civil discourse. If you're going to be biased against anything, be biased against biases! Everyone has experiences that shape our opinions on various issues, but when we give these too much weight and let them have undue influence on our discourse, we have failed to reach our full potential as conversants. Self-reflection can help us avoid this.

Q: My friends have told me that I am biased. I find it kind of offensive. How do I respond?

A: Listen to them! It is always important to listen to others' critiques and criticisms. Criticisms given with good intentions are always appreciated and helpful, but even criticisms said in malice are worth listening to and sifting through the dirt of the harsh tone in search of the gold of truth. Sometimes, critiques are right, and it's necessary to take stock of our flaws regularly. We may not see our biases, and someone else's point of view is essential. Even if they are wrong in their point, it is still worth looking at why people associate that bias with you and what you should do about that. Use this as an opportunity for self-reflection!

Q: But we aren't strapped into caves like Plato said, right?

A: Literally? No—at least most of us aren't. Figuratively? There's a lot to be said for Plato's Cave. We are all chained down in our lives in some ways. We have familial responsibilities and professional obligations. Some of us have religious, political, or social affiliations. There are all kinds of connections that limit our abilities to see the entire world around us. These obligations constrain our time, energies, and beliefs. And while we happily and freely give in to these restrictions, we can live well by recognizing the biases that result from the caves we live in and the chains that hold us down.

Plato's Cave allegory is just that—an allegory. It's meant to show that humans often assume things are true without question or further analysis. So, while we all might be "metaphorically" trapped in caves, we also all have the power to escape. How? By practicing self-reflection, engaging in civil discourse, and opening our minds to new ideas. This way, you're not "trapped" in the illusions of your own reality but able to live and think freely.

ACCEPTING ONE'S FLAWS AND CRITICISMS

Just as we talked earlier about subjectivity in the Plato's Cave story, let's talk about our own self-judgment. The truth is that we cannot be fair judges of how right or wrong we are. One aspect of subjectivity is our inability to be right 100 percent of the time. We are incapable of being completely correct, logically minded human beings who purely respond to things using perfect facts and data. The fact is, many of our viewpoints stem from emotions rather than reason. That presents a problem in and of itself. We are imperfect beings who get things wrong—frequently. However, it's in our nature to want to be right. No one wakes up and thinks, *I'd like to be wrong today.* Instead, we use the rational elements of our brain to come to conclusions that we believe to be right. Oftentimes, our emotions come first. In some cases, even if we can't find a rational way to be correct—be it through insecurity, lack of awareness, or something more sinister—we alter our view of reality to make ourselves *feel* right, even if we are objectively wrong.

The concepts of ego and unity consciousness have been studied by philosophers and psychologists throughout history. The ego, often associated with the work of Sigmund Freud and Carl Jung, is viewed as the part of the mind that is focused on the self and its needs. It is driven by ambition, self-interest, and the desire for power and control. The ego is seen as the "I" or self-centered part of one's mind that prioritizes one's own needs, pleasure, and enhancement to the exclusion of others and is selfishly ambitious. It sees relationships in terms of threat or no threat.

On the other hand, unity consciousness is the idea that all living things are connected and that individuals should strive for a sense of oneness and interconnectedness. This concept is often associated with spiritual and religious teachings, which promote compassion, love, and respect for all beings. It is a level of vibration that goes beyond the self and reaches the heart and souls of all beings and existence. Unity consciousness manifests as the sense of oneness, compassion, love, and respect, both for human beings and for nature.

In the scenario of being trapped on a deserted island, the ego would prioritize the self-preservation, such as fleeing from a tiger, while unity consciousness would consider the interconnectedness of all living things and the importance of preserving life, leading to a more compassionate and holistic approach to the situation. In a society, the ego can drive individuals to prioritize their own needs and desires, leading to a focus on competition and the desire to be "right." In contrast, unity consciousness promotes a sense of inter-connectedness and mutual understanding, leading to cooperation and a focus on the greater good.

If an ego brags about chopping down a tree in the forest, and no one is there to hear it, can we consider it a humblebrag? The ego plays a significant role in our desire to be right in the eyes of other people. When you're proven right, you get the chance to (metaphorically, I hope) beat your chest and display your pride in front of others. When you're proven wrong, others can slay (again, metaphorically, I hope) you mercilessly for it. While it feels pretty good to be the one celebrating in the first instance, it doesn't feel great to be the one in the wrong. It's better to be humble when you're right or wrong, and take the necessary steps to correct your thoughts and behavior accordingly.

Boosting your ego by proving that you're right can quickly turn into a continual, unproductive competition with everyone. You might even get to the point of keeping score. This can become especially problematic in interpersonal relationships. Social interaction isn't about scoring "points" by being right in arguments with your friends, family, romantic partners, or even strangers. You're the only one who cares about all those past times you were right and others were wrong. While it may feel good in the moment, it can do untold damage to your relationships with other people. Think about it: is it worth being right if no one can stand being around you?

This point-scoring can find its way into other interactions beyond discussions of right or wrong. If a couple is having a discussion, and someone says, "I always take the trash out; you do nothing but lie there!" they are likely engaging in disingenuous dialogue and point scoring—especially if you have clear evidence to the contrary. It's important to see yourself and others in a more positive light and not always think of you being in the right and the other being in the wrong.

Another factor in our desire to be right is the fear of criticism. While constructive criticism can be palatable and useful for self-improvement, harsh criticism can sting—though it can still be useful. However, the fear of criticism causes so many people to abandon their dreams before they've even started. At some point in your life, you've probably heard some motivational quote like "You can't succeed if you don't try." However, actually "trying" increases the risk of being wrong, thereby increasing the risk of being criticized. As a result, many people simply don't try because they don't want to be wrong, look foolish, or become the target of criticism. They stick to the things they already know and never venture into unknown territory.

The previous example is the protective nature of the ego. The ego tells you to stay inside, to not go for a promotion, or to not go on that vacation. It tends to be fear driven. *What if you look ridiculous in front of your peers? What if you get hurt?* It creates scenarios that simultaneously keep you safe and also hold you back. It's why Swiss psychoanalyst and prolific author Carl Jung quipped, "The question is, of course, what do you feel to be your task? Where your fear is, there is your task!" If something is holding you back, and that something is just your ego's fear, pushing through it can lead to almost incalculable growth.

I grew up thinking I had to be right at all costs, with little self-reflection. Maybe that's a competitive mindset suited to sports, but it's not suited to interpersonal communication. Perhaps it's how society teaches young men to act, or maybe it was just my traditional upbringing. Until the age of seventeen, though, I had the mindset that I needed to be right, no matter what. It was all or nothing for me. I was totally unable to see other people's points of view because I was convinced of my own prowess. I thought everything I did was the most logical and the most correct. In conversations, I didn't sit and listen to what others were saying; I would just think of ways I could dive in and disagree with them, demonstrating my intellectual abilities (and, unintentionally, lack of self-worth). Eventually, this made me into a rather negative person—yes, I was *that* kind of guy. I regularly called things out as I saw them, even exaggerating stories just to be right. I was overconfident in my wit rather than questioning myself productively. My ego was large, and I wasn't much of a joy to be around. I thought that me being right was the highest value rather than valuing the nature of truth (and subjective truth) in and of itself.

Once, after being argumentative and critical without provocation, a friend defeatedly asked me, "Why are you so negative all the time?" I responded how I usually did, by arguing against it, but as soon as I lifted my finger and took an inhale, my hand went back down. The words that would usually spew out turned into mud and slid back down my throat. I gulped—and had nothing to say. Then it hit me—I had to change my mindset. I focused on self-reflection through meditation, assessed my personal values, and established my desired impact on the world. I put effort into self-trust rather than self-confidence to foster deeper connection in my relationships with others. I reoriented my tone and interactive style to bring more positivity and civility to my personal and business relationships. I decided to stop thinking I was right, bar none, and started thinking of myself as one person with a contribution to make—and even more to receive from the people I spoke with.

The most important step was realizing that I didn't want to be that negative person anymore. I wanted people to *want* to be around me, to desire my company, to know that I saw them as equals and didn't act like I was better, smarter, or funnier than them. I needed to change my way of thinking. Part of this, though, meant learning how to accept errors—mine and those of others—which is something we are rarely taught how to do. The ability to admit being wrong, or even just feeling open to the possibility of being mistaken, is crucial to improving discourse. Acknowledging being wrong allows someone else the opportunity to be right.

In retrospect, the brash confidence of my teenage years likely stemmed from a need to fit in while in school and around other young men who would push their toxic masculinity with little understanding of their impact. I was raised by very strong women; in my early life it was my grandmothers and my mother, then followed by my sister and friends in school. Kids called me "gay" as an insult throughout my early years, likely pushing me to numb the side of me that cared for others and would entertain civil discourse. I felt the need to be definitive, overly confident, and outspoken.

While these are in part personality traits that still exist and come up from time to time in moments of instinct or necessity, I believe that these traits are not who I am. Toxic masculinity not only creates a toxic atmosphere in which men don't know how to admit when they're wrong or apologize, but it also makes it easier for men to assume women are "wrong" because men incorrectly associate them as less confident and definitive. The implications of this often unconscious sexism have appeared in numerous situations, from business to politics and beyond.

Throughout the years, I have become much more conscious of it, especially in the workplace. It amazes me to work with my sister as a co-founder, and consistently witness ideas, comments, or suggestions she makes go unrecognized. Of course, many of her suggestions only resurface later, and they receive praise because they are suggested by a man. Toxic masculinity may not be new to many of you, but I share this story to exemplify that vulnerability is strength.

Justin Baldoni, author of the book *Man Enough,* talks about his journey in writing a book that explores toxic masculinity:

> What led me on [this] journey is that I was tired of hurting people. And I was tired of hurting myself. I was tired of putting on masks and armor that I didn't know I was wearing. I was tired of acting different based on who I was around. I was tired of puffing up my chest when I was around certain men that I felt insecure around or women.[1]

Justin's dedication to showing the importance of dropping the bravado in pursuit of a more compassionate approach is part of what inspired me to pursue civility in all that I do. Of course, it's possible to be a man and conduct civil discourse. Countless people throughout history demonstrate that. Having toxic masculinity, however, makes civil discourse impossible.

Being right, angry, adamant, and dismissive creates a coat of armor around you—but that armor doesn't make you more agile or braver. It makes you clunky, and it makes it harder to connect with others. That bravado actually stops you from knowing yourself, uncovering your pain, and realizing who you truly are. You're not a better person when trying to convince everyone else of your strength. You're a better person when you show you're an authentic human with a range of emotions.

When you strip yourself of that bulky armor, you can be the acceptable face of an emotional state many are afraid to admit to being in. For me, that's strength.

When someone doesn't know how to admit when they're wrong, or is adamant in their rightness, it makes discourse impossible. Unproductive debates often ensue. Shouting matches emerge. No minds change, but adrenaline and cortisol flow through the system, causing inflammation in the body and anger in the mind. This creates room for debates to turn into glorified pissing contests. Who displays the most strength? Which person shows the most conviction in their beliefs? Who seems more powerful? Arguments come down to these futile questions that don't bring the discussion toward the truth but simply help to crown a winner and a loser.

Instead, we have to accept that we have been wrong in the past, we may be wrong now, and we will most certainly be wrong again at some point in the future. The same is true for anyone else in the conversation, and that's part of why civil discourse is so essential: Anyone can learn when they are wrong and have their mind changed to reach the truth, or at least a mutually beneficial situation. The first step is acknowledging that you aren't always right and that criticisms or critiques of your positions are sometimes very justified and helpful. Once you've cultivated the ability to recognize fault in yourself, evaluate it. Then go about changing it. You have the power to engage in actual discourse!

JAPANESE APPROACHES TO ACCEPTING FLAWS

Earlier in this chapter, we explored the idea of biases and subjectivity by embracing the Western philosophy of Plato's Cave. To explore how we can accept and acknowledge our mistakes and misconceptions, we engage with an aspect of Eastern thought: Japanese philosophy. These ideas on meditation, cultivation of the perfect, and self-improvement are drawn from the traditional Japanese religion and worldview, Shinto, as well as Buddhism and other meditative traditions.

Japanese art and culture emphasize perfection in many forms: poetry, origami, calligraphy, bonsai and flower arrangement, and even the samurai mentality. These are all ways of accepting the idea that practice allows for improvement. They help us remember that perfection is achievable by recognizing flaws as opportunities for improvement. A good way to think of this is by approaching tasks with the fool's mindset. If you always think of yourself as the fool (or beginner) and you have a chance to "play" with new ideas, and accept that you're sometimes going to fail but it'll make you better, you will consistently improve in your endeavors (and be less afraid to engage in new ones).

As another example, let's look at the Japanese concept of *kaizen*. The term roughly translates to "continuous improvement" and is frequently implemented in business environments. In essence, kaizen refers to change implemented at every point within an organization, from the CEO and upper management to lower-level workers. But you can use kaizen beyond the boardroom. You can strive to continually improve yourself on *all* levels by accepting mistakes and acknowledging when you are wrong. You can exercise this type of self-reflection within personal growth and family dynamics. This could also be called a "growth mindset." It means you're accepting that you're not a finished product—that you can still grow like a plant toward the light of understanding and self-knowledge.

Adopting the idea that you are not perfect but can always strive toward perfection is a way to accept being wrong as an opportunity. It's a chance to make something even more beautiful or productive. I'll discuss ways to apply kaizen to civil discourse later in the book.

Japanese culture has another mentality to help us accept our wrongness and strive to learn from it: Zen Buddhism—a philosophical tradition that builds upon the Buddhism that originated in India. It is useful for people of any religion or belief system because Buddhism teaches the importance of slowing down, reflecting on one's own life, and treating others with compassion and civility. It encourages sitting in addition to quiet reflection on serious questions—from the pragmatic to the philosophical—in the hope of better understanding ourselves and our world. It comes from quieting yourself, being still, and stopping the inner chatter (*monkey brain!*) and taking on the role of the observer. So breathe slowly, and allow a level of understanding to emerge from that tumult of to-do lists, emails, and looming weekend plans.

When we draw from these two mindsets—kaizen and Japanese Zen Buddhism—we can use their various tools to accept ourselves when we are wrong. They let us emphasize openness and civility so we are better equipped to listen and consider flaws in our views. They can stop us from overly identifying with our opinions, allowing us the freedom to breathe and move to new mindsets when confronted with new information.

So find a comfortable spot as we talk about meditation: that time of quiet contemplation and calmness during which we can relax and reach more profound, more fulfilling conclusions about our thoughts.

The first tenet of self-reflection through meditation is solitude. It's difficult to uncover truths about yourself when external stimuli surround you. While some people are better at drowning out the noise than others, it's best to practice self-reflection in a quiet environment where distractions are limited and especially where no one will bother you. Even if you only have ten free minutes to yourself each day, try to use that time to reflect quietly. Turn off your phone and set it aside. Ask your loved ones for some time without interruption. Sit comfortably with good posture—legs crossed, spine straight, slightly tucked chin—close your eyes, and inhale deeply and slowly through your nose. Hold it for four seconds, and exhale even longer.

Breathing is an essential part of meditation. In fact, meditation is often essential breathwork before anything else. Hop onto YouTube and search for a "guided meditation" if you feel you need some assistance. There are a host of apps out there, too. When you're ready, focus on the topics you want to think about when meditating.

Finding time to meditate can be extremely difficult, and I know that firsthand. As a CEO and leader of multiple companies, things feel like they are always moving—I constantly feel like a rubber band getting pulled in every direction. For those with kids, I know it's nearly impossible to find quiet time, and students, well, you have enough distractions as it is. But do what you can to meditate and self-reflect—before the day's challenges and obligations storm you like shoppers at a Black Friday sale.

When it comes to meditation, one minute is better than zero. *Something* is an improvement from *nothing*. Although I encourage you to aim for more. A single, deep, mindful breath is beneficial. The trick is to just add more into your day. Starting with self-reflection allows you to set a tone for the day—one of self-trust, calm, and balance. This is the best way to ensure you will be ready for civil discourse right at the start of your morning.

When you have struggled to maintain civility in discourse or experienced uncivil treatment during a discussion, it is worth meditating later to reflect on the potential biases, emotions, and problems that disrupted the conversation. Ask yourself, "How could these problems have been avoided?" "What can I do better in the future?" "How can I foster a better spirit of civility in future discussions?"

Meditation allows us to recognize where our values and biases exist. Through breathing and thought meditation, I was personally able to accept some of the criticism faced by *The Doe*. I evaluated my values and how those shaped my position in discourse with both readers and my team.

Meditation also allows us to visualize without distraction. We can visualize and learn from previous success, building self-trust. We can also visualize what future success would look like and understand how we can take our own kaizen steps—seeking to improve ourselves and move closer to the perfect success we'd dream of attaining. We can also visualize the things in our lives or subconscious that aren't serving us and that we need to deal with and unpack. We can ensure that we resolve what is buried within us as quiet reflection brings it to the surface.

Accepting Flaws
QUESTIONS AND ANSWERS

Q: Are there any books you'd suggest I read to learn more about meditating?

A: Meditating is one of the best ways to clear your mind and practice self-reflection. There are a multitude of books out there, but my personal favorite is S. N. Goenka's *The Art of Living: Vipassana Meditation*.[2] The Vipassana technique has its roots in India, where it has been practiced for thousands of years.

Q: What are some questions I should think about while meditating that will help me be a better participant in civil discourse?

A: To some degree, the questions you ask yourself in moments of quiet meditation will depend on your personal characteristics and circumstances. That said, you can begin by asking more general questions that will help lead you down the path toward self-discovery. Here are a few good questions to get you started:

• Sometimes we take advantage of people in our lives. What behaviors have I engaged in lately that might be doing a disservice to others?

- Have I been dishonest with myself? What were the consequences of that? Why might I have done this, and what could I do to avoid this in the future?

- Have I been honest with others? What situations or behaviors have led to dishonesty with others? How did that impact them, and how should I remedy the situation?

- Am I acting like the kind of person that I want to be? If not, how can I change?

- What are the goals that I've set for myself? How have I been striving for them recently?

- How am I behaving when I talk with others? What impact does that behavior have? Are those the actions and reactions I want?

- How am I bringing emotions into my discourse in unproductive ways?

- How did I feel after the last time I talked to this person or engaged in this kind of conversation?

Q: What are some tips for integrating self-reflection into a busy schedule?

A: You may think that you have no free time, but everyone has the same number of hours every day. It comes down to how you prioritize your life. Whether you take a break during your workday or you set aside a few minutes for self-reflection before you go to sleep, you must make it a priority. If you don't treat self-reflection as an essential activity, you'll never find the time to do it. So look at self-reflection as a necessary part of your day. No matter how busy your schedule may be, you can find a way to insert a few minutes to contemplate and reflect on your daily routine.

SUMMARY

In this chapter, we've explored how self-reflection can help us reach a clearer state of mind to engage in civil discourse. Sometimes, we have to take a step back and reflect on our values and biases to understand why we behave in certain ways and what we can do to add value to our interactions with others.

Remember these points to engage in meaningful self-reflection, which are applicable to many life situations, including open-minded conversations.

- Self-reflection is an opportunity to recognize our subjectivity and our biases to better understand our own position in any discussion.
- Plato's *Allegory of the Cave* reminds us that we are often too constrained in our lives to see all the details of the world around us. We must be vigilant about questioning our perspective. Remembering that others have their perspectives and showing compassion for others' points of view will allow for more civil discourse.
- It is difficult, and sometimes even painful, to admit when we are not right. We like to believe that we are, but that's simply

unrealistic. We are all wrong sometimes, and accepting that reality is a primary step to ensuring discourse stays civil when someone disagrees with you.

- We can draw from Japanese ideas of contemplation and pursuit of continuous improvement to combat our tendency to always assume we are right. We do not have to see misunderstandings as flaws but as opportunities to perfect ourselves and our discursive styles.

FINAL QUESTIONS AND ANSWERS

Q: I've never spent any time self-reflecting, and it sounds difficult. I'm not quite sure where to start. Can you provide some tips?

A: Self-reflection is not tricky—even if it seems that way at first—and everyone is capable of doing it. Start with the meditation techniques I've discussed and with the prompts listed in previous question sections. As time passes, you will improve at self-reflection. Even starting with something simple, like thinking about how you interacted with someone earlier in the day, will help you learn more about yourself. It's okay to start self-reflection as a novice. You'll grow more confident in it over time.

Q: I'm busy and my mind is always spinning, so I'm not sure I will be good at self-reflecting. What should I do if I try and fail?

A: Not everyone feels comfortable with self-reflection, but that doesn't mean you aren't "good" at it, or that you'll fail. Any time you can spend on it will be rewarding. First, try to identify obstacles you might have. For instance, do you have difficulty finding a quiet space or time? Try to isolate yourself at a slow time of day and remove distractions. Do you get distracted too easily? Physically place your distractions away, and then create a list of topics you want to focus on in a given self-reflection session. Not sure what to think about? Choose questions and thought exercises beforehand, from this book or elsewhere, to guide you. We struggle with one aspect of the process of self-reflection, not the reflection itself, and once you address that aspect, you will have more productive sessions.

Q: Is there a point when I can consider myself done with self-reflecting?

A: We are never done self-reflecting—that is why it's such a great tool. Like meditation, self-reflection gets easier with practice. We all have egos and mental "blocks" to overcome, so there's no shame in not being great at self-reflection right from the start. Just like it takes time to develop biases, it also takes time to undo them! You are always changing, growing, and adapting, and so there are still opportunities to look at your current beliefs, behaviors, and situations to evaluate yourself. There is always a need for self-reflection.

Chapter Two
Intention

Think of every conversation like it's about to date your daughter: question the *intent*. While you cannot always know the intent of another person, you can—and must—work to understand your own intent.

There are many possible intentions you might hold upon entering discourse. You might engage out of pure intellectual curiosity or a desire to learn something new. Alternatively, you might engage with someone to voice your own opinions and demand that you be heard. Your intent may also come from the desire to defeat or outsmart your "opponent." And in many instances, you might engage with someone by accident as a seemingly inconsequential conversation turns into a debate, in which case your intent may be innocuous.

You might think that the fundamental barrier to civil discourse is a lack of intent, or even the presence of bad intentions. But the actual problem occurs when there is a lack of *well-defined* intent. Misunderstanding is the real gap between discussants. Sometimes you might enter a conversation at a leisurely pace, without a care about what happens or where you go. This is not necessarily a bad thing. You don't always need a map when you go on a walk. However, if you bring some idea of which direction you'd like to go, your conversations will be more productive. You need some awareness of your intent—a compass of sorts—to pursue the ultimate goal of civil discourse: *finding truth or producing mutually beneficial results.*

As a young teen selling turtles, I realized I had to be very aware of my intentions in every conversation. I was still a child, and I had a bunch of reptiles growing under my parents' roof. This meant choosing my words carefully and hiding my symptoms if I ended up with salmonella after sucking one end of a tube to get the last of the water out of the tank (nothing that regular hydration and a bit of bedrest couldn't fix, though). If my parents came to me concerned about the reptile farm festering in my bedroom or the floods I'd accidentally created, I couldn't think of the conversation as something I needed to *win*. I had to be intentional about the conversation—and help both parties arrive at a place where both of us gained something.

"Where did these new turtles come from?" my mom would ask.

At first, that question could make me defensive. My instinct would be to say "Why does it matter?" Of course, that response would not help the situation. If I thought about my intention in that conversation, I would know that a response of "Who cares?" would not help either party achieve their goals. I needed to recognize not just my intentions but my mother's as well. If I could recognize hers *and* mine, then I could bring the conversation where I wanted it.

My mom, ultimately, cared about me and my well-being. As much as it sometimes annoyed me, that was *her* intention in the conversation. A good response on my part went something like "I got the turtles from a breeder in San Francisco. This one is a clown red-eared slider. You can tell by the brightly colored shell."

That sort of response helped ease my mom's concerns. I wasn't dismissive. I understood where she was coming from as well as where I was coming from, and I tailored my conversation to that.

THE CONSEQUENCES OF ILL-DEFINED INTENT

Without clear, conscious intent, any number of consequences can arise. Imagine you're going into a job interview at the local bakery, Mr. Charlie's Cupcake Emporium. Most people would have an obvious intention: get a job! But that's a bit vague, isn't it? Getting a job can't be boiled down to one statement. Simply planning to "get a job" would be like a cookbook writer writing "bake cupcakes" under the recipe for cupcakes. They would need to be more specific. They would have to talk about the ingredients and the measurements. The cookbook writer would need to tell the reader at what temperature to set the oven, and how long the cupcakes would need to be in there.

If you walked into the back room of Mr. Charlie's Cupcake Emporium, telling yourself your intention was *to get a job,* you wouldn't know how to answer Mr. Charlie when he asks why you want to work with cupcakes. You would stare blankly at him when he asks you what your strengths are and blink in confusion when he inquires about your cupcake-baking skills.

That's why more focused intentions are important. If you went into Mr. Charlie's Cupcake Emporium intending to highlight your skills and share your knowledge and love of baking, you would be much better prepared. You could actually tell Mr. Charlie that you "love seeing a smile on someone's face when they bite into a baked good," or impress the dessert mogul by describing the recipe for lemon cream cupcakes that you've perfected over the years.

Defining intentions is a necessary step in improving communications at any level, not just interactions where you are trying to gain something as concrete as a job. Let's take a step back for a second. Think about a smaller-scale example where ill-defined intent has affected an interaction of your own. Maybe it was a simple conversation with your significant other or a parent. How was intention relevant to you in that moment?

Ill-Defined Intent
QUESTIONS AND ANSWERS

Q: How can I know if my own intentions are ill-defined?

A: Whether you're starting a business or engaging in a conversation, you should always ask yourself the same question: *Do I know exactly what I want?* Sometimes, you may need the opinions of others to help you gain clarity on the subject. However, if you want to know whether or not you are going into a situation or endeavor with ill-defined intentions, you can examine your goals and personal interests to see if there is any room to better define your intent—regardless of the circumstances.

Admittedly, I understand that conversations are plentiful in our day-to-day lives, and most are not planned in advance. They're spontaneous or creative in nature. Sure, rigidly asking yourself, *Do I know exactly what I want?* in every circumstance would be a little robotic. But picking more broad intentions, such as "Be friendly to people," will prime you to have better-defined intentions.

Q: What can I do to focus my intent?

A: You know how children tend to ask endless chains of questions until their parents or teachers run out of answers? Well, this is exactly what you should do with yourself. For example, let's say you're going to a friend's house and you know they want to talk to you about the previous weekend when you got annoyed at something they said and snapped. You might realize it wasn't really anything your friend did, but it was more of a result of your bad mood. First, ask yourself what you want to gain from the conversation. Then, ask yourself *why* you want to gain it. Then, ask yourself *why* that is the reason that you want to gain it. Continue this process until you run out of answers. Essentially, if you keep asking yourself "why?" you will be able to focus your intent as much as possible.

Q: Is it wrong to go into a conversation with no intent at all?

A: Absolutely not! While ill-defined intentions can have negative consequences, no intent at all can often be a reflection of an open mind, which is an integral part of civil discourse. *Knowing you have no intent is in itself defining your intent*—allowing reason and polite argumentation to lead the way. Just be conscious of how your intent could begin to form as the conversation proceeds. You could end up unconsciously developing intentions that either diminish your ability to engage in discourse or even work against the interests of others.

IDENTIFYING BAD INTENTIONS

While it's relatively easy to identify good intentions and, to a lesser degree, ill-defined intentions, it's not always so easy to identify bad intentions. This is because bad intent is often the army hidden inside the Trojan Horse of "good" intent.

One need only look to Bangladeshi economist Muhammad Yunis for an example of good intentions that were later expanded, manipulated, and turned into something disastrous. In 1976, Yunis created the concept of "microloans" by providing loans to local women who would not qualify for traditional bank loans. These loans were then used to buy the materials needed for artisans to create and sell their wares or to open small restaurants and other service-oriented businesses. The endeavor turned out to be a huge success, allowing Yunis to open the Grameen Bank, which raised hundreds of thousands of women and families out of poverty by issuing over 8 million microloans.

Over time, Yunis's idea spread across the world, with lending institutions adopting the practice particularly in rural or impoverished regions. This accelerated when he and Grameen Bank were awarded the 2006 Nobel Peace Prize, emphasizing the ties between ending poverty and promoting political stability. However, Yunis began his endeavor with the intent to lift people (particularly women) out of poverty. For this reason, he set very low interest rates that were easier to pay back over time. It allowed him to profit from his idea without needing to take advantage of some of the world's most disadvantaged populations.

Naturally, not everyone had the same good intentions as Yunis. While microloans from lenders in impoverished areas seemed to be providing funds to those most in need, many did so using extremely high interest rates, especially in Mexico and India. Much like the predatory payday lenders common in impoverished areas throughout the United States, these institutions forced millions of families into perpetual cycles of debt, as they could not afford to pay back the usurious loans. Thus, the commercialization of microloans ultimately defeated the good intentions of the initial concept.

In this situation, it was clear that for-profit microfinance institutions had bad intentions. They knew that poor families could not make the payments on loans with high interest rates, but they issued the loans anyway. It is not always so easy to tell when individual intentions are bad, though. So how do you identify bad intentions in yourself and others?

To begin, it is usually easier to identify your own bad intentions than it is to identify someone else's. As noted in the previous Q&A section, you can often illuminate and define your own intent by asking yourself *why* you want to pursue certain goals or maintain certain intentions. Once you have a greater sense of clarity on the subject, try to take an objective approach. Is your intent self-serving? Does it do anything to help others? Will it contribute to civil discourse insofar as it moves you closer to the truth or mutually beneficial results?

Generally speaking, if your intent only benefits you—especially at the expense of others—there is a strong chance that it is objectively "bad." This is often the case if you are concealing your intentions.

Say you've invited a friend over and he just so happens to be a handy mechanic. Say his name is Otto. Imagine that as soon as Otto comes over, you start talking about your annoying car issues. "It's such a pain, too! I have to get to the post office to get my passport photo taken," you might say. Maybe you could even unsubtly droop your head in dismay.

Good-natured Otto does exactly what you expected and spends two hours fixing it. "Oh, wow, thanks, Otto! You really didn't have to do that," even though all the parts he needed were miraculously waiting for him in the garage.

Furthermore, when it's time to eat, you rush poor Otto through dinner, making up an excuse that you're tired. Gotta be refreshed for that passport photo! Clearly, you had bad intentions in this situation. You invited Otto over so you could benefit.

How do we ensure that our intentions are properly defined? If you really wanted your mechanical friend to come help you, and you really had "good" intentions, you would have asked Otto outright if he could fix it, and offered to pay him for his time. This would have been creating an honest interaction based on your true intentions so that he knew exactly what to expect.

That is treating someone like a human *being* rather than a human *doing*.

For the purposes of identifying intentions, we might think of "good" as anything that moves discourse closer to honesty, truth, and benefits for all. Alternatively, something that is "bad" does the opposite: it threatens to undermine discourse by moving it closer to deceit, falsity, and benefits for only a few.

It would be great if you could use the same strategies previously outlined to identify bad intentions in others, but unfortunately, discourse does not work that way. People, particularly those who want to "win" a discussion, will likely try very hard to hide their true intentions like you did with Otto. Someone with bad intentions may alter answers to paint themselves more favorably, and they may even outright lie. In any case, you will often have to trust the other person to some degree, even if there's a part of you that thinks they may not be arguing in good faith.

A good-faith argument occurs when someone acts with honest intent, speaks clearly about what it is they are arguing, and does not hold the other person to an impossible standard. Those arguing in good faith do not look for "gotcha" moments to score if the other person slips up. They faithfully represent the opposing argument to the best of their ability.

Unsurprisingly, bad faith arguments are the opposite. They twist and conceal intention and misrepresent opposing arguments. If I told you I didn't like pizza, and you were arguing in bad faith, you might accuse me of hating all Italian culture rather than taking what I said as what I meant—I just don't like pizza.

So what is the good-intentioned key to the bad-intentioned lock in a discussion? Try reading your counterpart(s) during a discourse for signs of bad intentions. Naturally, the exact process for doing this will vary from one situation to another. However, asking questions is your best tool for identifying intent in others. You may not always get the truth, but you can use questions to evaluate the viewpoint, personality, and various other aspects of the other person. The more you come to understand them, the greater the chance that you will identify the "goodness" of their intentions. However, as in the pizza example, your questions must be well-intentioned. Don't rely on "gotcha" questions to proverbially push your discussant into a corner. If you ask good questions, you can help someone else clarify what their intention is. It doesn't matter if you agree or disagree as long as you are trying to better learn their position and where they're coming from.

Identifying Bad Intentions
QUESTIONS AND ANSWERS

Q: What do I do if I can't always tell if someone else has bad intentions?

A: You're never going to know exactly what someone's intentions are 100 percent of the time. You can only improve your own level of judgment. We cannot train ourselves to be perfect, but we can ensure we have better intuition when it comes to human behavior (especially behavior of people we know).

If you're speaking to someone you do not know (or do not know very well), you will likely struggle to tell if their intentions are good or not. As a result, most discourse will begin without a clear idea of where everyone's intentions lie. This doesn't mean that civil discourse is a hopeless endeavor; it just means that you have to extend a degree of trust to the other person and ensure that you are going into the discussion with good intentions.

Q: Can civil discourse still happen if one or more people have bad intentions?

A: Yes, but civility is much more difficult. This is because you will constantly have to work to move the conversation back to a place of truth and good intent. You can't force someone to act against their own self-interest or stop having bad intentions, but you *can* drive the tone of the conversation—something we'll discuss further in Chapter 3. Therefore, civil discourse can happen if you insist on pursuing good intentions at all times.

Q: What resources can help with identifying the intent of others?

A: It can be difficult to read someone's intent from their words and tone, especially if they are being deliberately misleading or even calculating. However, all humans have core microexpressions—little, unconscious movements of the face and body—that convey real meanings and intentions. Like a poker player's "tells," microexpressions are subtle signs you can learn to read to reveal the intentions of others.

Paul Ekman, an anthropologist who has studied the phenomenon, has written many books and articles and has done interviews in which he provides insight into how you can learn to pick up on subtle cues. In fact, in his and his co-contributor Wallace Friesen's Facial Coding System made in 1978, he posits that we have over 10,000 different expressions, many of which we understand subliminally. Ekman states, "You may know how a person is feeling before he or she knows. You may also be able to recognize that there is a chance a person is trying to diminish or conceal her expressions."[3] In other words, with a trained eye and the right intuition, you can understand if someone is being deceitful or not.

In *Telling Lies: Clues to Deceit in the Marketplace, Politics, and Marriage,* Ekman says, "No discussion of facial signs of deceit would be complete without considering one of the most frequent of all the facial expressions—smiles. They are unique among facial expressions. It takes but one muscle to show enjoyment, while most of the other emotions require the action of three to five muscles."[4] There are so many different things we do that reveal and conceal our emotions, and learning to be an astute observer from experts like Ekman can help you identify the intent of others and also help you be more aware of yourself.

CURBING INTELLECTUAL DISHONESTY

If you've ever tuned in to a news opinion program to see people with differing views debate each other or just opened your Twitter feed to catch up on the day's events, you know that intellectual dishonesty runs rampant in our culture. One of the reasons for this is the concept of "views." Intellectual dishonesty—through exaggeration, fearmongering, misrepresentation of alternative points of view, confirmation bias, and many other deceitful techniques—increases viewership. But also fear, disasters, and other negative news can increase viewership. In a way, this makes sense. What would you be more likely to stop and watch: an exciting train heist or two people having an honest discussion over lunch about how much they like flowers? This use of disaster to drive ratings is evident in the fact that, while otherwise declining, the three major US news networks (CNN, Fox, and MSNBC) all saw significant viewership increases in 2020 due to the COVID-19 pandemic.

However, it's more than COVID that has led to a breakdown in discourse. It is evident beyond just news programs. For example, a court found[5] that MSNBC anchor Rachel Maddow's viewers understand she offers opinion and exaggeration rather than facts. Tucker Carlson, the popular Fox News anchor, admitted[6] on the YouTube podcast *The Rubin Report* that he "sometimes lies" on his show.

It's not just traditional news platforms that push misinformation on people to claw for viewership and profit. You can see this on various YouTube channels and other video- and podcast-hosting sites on the Internet. Intellectual dishonesty has practically become an institution, like religion or sports. This "Game of Intellectual Dishonesty" is especially popular in the political realm. With increased scrutiny on people's public and private lives, *rightness* is sometimes the only thing the players have to feel like they've scored a goal. In this messy sport, often the only way to achieve that is through stretching the truth. The key lies in identifying bad-faith actors and evaluating when they are acting dishonestly. Even if someone is not outright lying, they may be concealing the truth or bending reality to fit their argument or narrative.

Along with the aforementioned characteristics of bad-faith actors, intellectual dishonesty often comes in the form of purposefully obfuscating an issue by pretending to answer questions and causing confusion with "word salad" statements. For example, if you ask someone, "How do you feel about rising gas prices?" and they work for a gas company, a word salad response would be something like "Well prices are something that goes up and down, and there's the obtuse nature of the price of everything that rises and falls like a boat going out in the ocean. I feel there's a reason why we're on this planet, and we have an existential thing to reckon with that's beyond our comprehension in the natural order, such is the meaning of strange economies." Confused? That's the point—it's nonsensical and doesn't answer the question. That salad could use some dressing and maybe some croutons, if you ask me.

When people do serve you a word salad, it is hard to continue the conversation in a meaningful way. How do you respond to nonanswers or nonsensical remarks? This gives bad-faith actors greater power to move the discourse in the direction that best serves their goals.

Another meal in the same food group as word salad is a technique called "gish gallop." This is when an individual overwhelms the other person with an assortment of fact-like statements, quick speaking, and multiple arguments all at once. Gish gallop tends to be disorienting. It makes it difficult to follow the argument because it pulls multiple threads to form a messy oral tapestry. It is yet another hallmark of intellectual dishonesty.

Intellectual honesty means pursuing the truth regardless of whether or not it serves your interests or goals. With civil discourse, the best course of action is not to fight fire with fire because all that does is lead to a larger blaze. In other words, you shouldn't counter lies and manipulation with more lies. Instead, curb intellectual dishonesty by continually and persistently stating what is true. This forces bad-faith actors to confront their intellectual dishonesty, though they usually won't give in easily. You might have to ask many questions to understand why they are being dishonest and how they think it contributes to the conversation. Remember, if you take a harsh approach to confronting someone, they can easily become defensive. If you push too hard, you'll be unlikely to yield positive, constructive conversational results. Defensiveness—as we discussed earlier in this book—tends to reinforce viewpoints and, in this case, will likely just increase intellectual dishonesty.

When my parents divorced, it changed the trajectory of my life. And until recently, I realized that I wasn't being honest about my parents in the storytelling of my life—specifically, my father's background of being a successful entrepreneur. In my journey, I have tended to omit him from much of the narrative because to be compared to him was to undermine my own work—or at least that's what it felt like to me. People saw what my father had achieved and would immediately assume I would be an ungrateful and unappreciative person. Or the conversation would completely pivot to a tangent about him. Thus, perhaps in a rebellion or perhaps in frustration, I would omit how powerful my dad's influence had been in my life.

At first, I did not want to be like him because I did not want to be the family member constantly working and unavailable, like he was when I was growing up. This was my version of rebellion, I suppose. I wanted to be a farmer, to work in agriculture, and create a more humane food industry. But here I am, a tech founder and entrepreneur like him. Thanks, Dad.

In 2022, a team member at one of my companies challenged me with a poignant question after we got off a partner pitch call—"Why do you never bring your dad into your story?" This gave me pause. My answer was that I didn't want to use my dad's name and his success to give me undeserved leverage. I didn't want to benefit from nepotism. But that question also sparked an "aha" moment. Not being honest about my dad's journey was hurting me, the authenticity of my story, and my goals. It was awkward to leave him out of my story, especially since I spoke often about how my mom shaped my life. I had to examine my intentions.

I had thought that leaving him out was helpful. But it wasn't—it wasn't honest. Who was I to talk about the importance of civil discourse if I wasn't being 100 percent truthful whenever I talked about myself?

Intellectual dishonesty doesn't just rear its head in other people. It can show up in yourself as well. Remembering that can help you recognize the complexity of dishonesty and intent. My team members didn't confront my dishonesty by being hostile—they asked a genuine question in order to bring the truth to light.

Curbing intellectual dishonesty requires a lot of strength. It's harder than civil discourse taking place between two honest, willing participants. You may need to push yourself to the front of the conversation more than usual. Naturally, you should still listen to what the other person has to say, but if you see that dishonesty is taking over the conversation, you have to make a concerted effort to call out logical fallacies, misleading statements, half-truths, outright lies, inflated statistics, or remarks that are designed to evade or dilute the topic at hand. The skill lies in figuring out balance. Confront the dishonesty, but don't be disrespectful. Disrespect just breeds incivility and unproductivity. It's possible to speak with both respect and strength when pursuing the truth.

Curbing Intellectual Dishonesty
QUESTIONS AND ANSWERS

Q: How can I think about intention and curb intellectual dishonesty at the same time?

A: The truth is that you will have to adjust your listening and speaking behavior if you know that the other person is actively engaging in dishonest or manipulative behavior with unproductive intent. This doesn't mean you have to stop listening entirely, but it does mean that you will have to work harder to ensure that truth rules the discourse. Otherwise, you will find yourself in a one-sided conversation that is designed to deceive, confuse, or manipulate.

SUMMARY

In this chapter, we examined the concept of intent from multiple angles—from global disputes to conversations between two individuals. Intent is a tricky subject, whether you want to work on improving awareness of your own intentions or the intentions of others. Before you can attempt to pursue "good" intentions, you must first cultivate the ability to illuminate your intentions so that you can truly understand your actions. It can help you determine why you pursue certain goals. Once you have the ability to reflect on your intent, you can work on *improving* that intent. You will be able to identify intent in others to make civil discourse better for everyone.

Remember these points to ensure you have a solid grasp of your own intent and a better understanding of the intentions of others:

- Intent is the true, underlying purpose that drives your thoughts and actions. You must learn to push away self-deceit and get to the heart of your real pursuits to practice civil discourse.

- Bringing positive intent into your civil discourse is an important first step to productive conversation.

- Having no intent at all is still better than having ill-defined intent. Vague intentions can have disastrous consequences while no intent can actually allow you to practice civil discourse with an open mind that is unencumbered by personal goals or self-interest.

- You cannot always know the intent of others with 100 percent certainty. However, you can insist on pushing discourse toward a place of truth, honesty, and good intentions. Generally, if you go into discourse with no intent or with clear, good intentions, and you experience a great deal of resistance, it's a sign that the other person may have bad intentions or could be arguing in bad faith.

- Asking questions and listening to the answers intently are your greatest tools for identifying intent and helping ensure that civil discourse can happen.

FINAL QUESTIONS AND ANSWERS

Q: On some occasions, I've finished a conversation, and the other person will accuse me of having ill intentions. I thought I was being honest and fair and don't know where I went wrong. How can I better understand my own intent when I can't see this myself?

A: Self-awareness is a difficult practice to cultivate. You may think you are pursuing one thing when in reality, you are unconsciously pursuing something completely different. Consequently, practicing self-reflection—as we discussed in Chapter 1—and coming to know yourself can help you understand your own intent as much as possible. That said, if you still struggle to understand your own intent, you can actively work to engage in civil discourse without any intent beyond finding the truth or finding mutually beneficial results.

Additionally, intentions are rarely black and white. They can be, and often are, quite complex. You may have conflicting interests and intentions (for example, you might want to hear the other person out but also express your own opinion). Again, this can be resolved by asking yourself questions about the underlying reasons behind your pursuit of certain goals or actions. In doing so, you can have a better understanding of your intent and, if necessary, work to improve it for the sake of improving civil discourse. Reflection remains a core part of the process of meaningful civil discourse.

Chapter Three
Tone

Very few of us believe that reality TV actually depicts reality. Many shows, though, can provide a window for us to understand the art of human communication and tone. Many sitcoms, like *Friends* or *Cheers,* portray serious human experiences, but the characters rarely, if ever, lose their humorous attitude. Reality shows like *Real Housewives* also show intense human interaction, but if everyone maintained a calm, measured tone, there would be no viewership.

But one TV star in particular stands above the rest as a quintessential example of excellence in civil discourse—at least as far as tone is concerned. I'm talking about Mr. Rogers, a man who spent a lifetime being emotionally present for children across the nation without ever having to step into their homes. It wasn't just children he impacted, though. He helped generations of parents struggling to raise their children in a society that was quickly evolving with the opportunities and challenges of modern technology. Mr. Rogers taught a generation of children how to treat their neighbors, regardless of race or financial status, with calm and respect. He demonstrated interacting with a kind and authentic tone.

Mr. Rogers taught us that when our neighbor wins, we all win. When the person who shines your shoes, makes your coffee, or serves you at a restaurant has a positive interaction with you, then society evolves and progresses. He showed that even if the objectives of a moment in time are different from person to person, enjoying your time together can be the common ground you both share.

It's not worth making assumptions about others, as Mr. Rogers exemplifies. Throughout his show, Mr. Rogers chose selflessness over selfishness, civil discourse over rudeness, and humility over pride. He saw the importance in reflecting on how we approach the world, and not focusing on how others show up. So when we surprise people by being present, by being kind, or by seeking common ground, we advance society at the grassroots level.

Mr. Rogers was consistent on television for demonstrating how impactful a kind approach could be for the strengthening of relationships. Close your eyes and imagine his voice in your head. The very fact you can is a sign of how powerfully gentle and kind his tone was. His voice allowed for self-reflection and pause when discussing difficult subjects, and he practiced what he preached. I believe Mr. Rogers exemplified love of humans and love of the "other" better than anyone I've seen on television. Now, for the many generations of children and parents who watched *Mr. Rogers' Neighborhood* throughout the thirty-one seasons that aired, it's easy to see Mr. Rogers' authentic personality come through. One can't help but believe that his attention and care for every thirty-second relationship reached a level of saintliness—a once-in-a-century human who had an inhuman ability to calm the world.

However, to put such a person on a pedestal may be to assume that his ability to speak kindly is impossible for others to learn. While it may be easier for some, improving the way we speak and respond to others is attainable for everyone—not just those who have their own children's show or trolley tracks in their house.

This is to say that any human who embodies the ability to conduct civil discourse by speaking to people the way they want to be spoken to has likely spent years perfecting these skills. Conducting civil discourse means constantly working at being a better human for the people around you. It's essential to not worry about where you are today but rather where you can be *tomorrow*.

The pattern of being a better listener, a conversationalist, and practitioner of civil discourse is a lifelong process, and all each of us can do is improve every day. You don't become a Mr. Rogers overnight.

Have you ever had a friend or family member get angry at a remark you made that you thought was totally appropriate? If you have, it may have left you dumbfounded. Maybe you questioned why your statement made them so angry and got a response like: "It wasn't what you said, it was how you said it."

This situation happens all too often because people sometimes adopt a tone that reflects a less-than-desirable intention. The problem is, of course, that we cannot hear our own tone the way other people do. "Sure, whatever!" might sound like an agreeable assent to you, but it may come across as a sarcastic mumbling to your aunt. We don't interpret our own tone the same way others might. This is no one's fault but simply one of the challenges humans face as complex communicators.

Perhaps you're speaking to a coworker and you want to emphasize the urgency of hitting a deadline, so you speak with a tone that is more forceful than usual. Your coworker may misinterpret your words as hostile and accusatory, potentially making it even harder to work together as a team to accomplish shared goals. Maybe you intended to enter the conversation with calm confidence, but what came out of your mouth sounded more demanding, bordering on aggressive. Mastering tone can be very challenging, especially when emotions run high. Sometimes you may find yourself even trying to suppress your emotions when you speak. You've probably been in a situation that made you angry, but you knew that demonstrating anger through a harsh tone would not be productive. Often, anger elicits defensiveness and is reciprocated by the person or people you're talking to because we interpret anger as a threat. That's when it's best to compose yourself, take a deep breath, and remain calm to best deliver your message.

When it comes to working as a team on shared goals, cultivating a collaborative tone is essential for civil discourse. But other tones—understanding, firm, and light—will be necessary for different circumstances. It all depends on the nature of the conversation, the scenario you're in, and the topic at hand. Different tones won't mean the same thing for every person or every situation. At times, having a collaborative tone, for example, may require you to suppress the urge to show aggression, focus more on listening than speaking, or even change your body language. In any case, working on improving your tone and aligning it with the intention and goal of civil discourse will make it that much easier to engage in productive dialogues.

Turtles were not my only foray into biological entrepreneurship. As I mentioned earlier, at one point I wanted to be a farmer. Being part Iranian, the natural step was in growing and cultivating saffron.

It grows from saffron crocus, a plant with whitish-purple flowers. It's a crop that grows in many places around the globe and is easy to grow, but the *stigmas* you must pick from each flower make harvesting the spice very labor intensive.

Saffron and civil discourse might seem unconnected, but the technique of cultivation requires calm, Zen-like focus. You have to handpick three stigmas from each flower before putting each stigma on a tray and drying them over charcoal fires. And, as is any sort of agricultural endeavor, you have to learn to understand your plant. You have to be aware of yourself when you pick the stigma and dry it. Being too rough could destroy the plant. Ideally, you want the "style" to be a deep shade of red, which shows the quality of the saffron (without using colorful dyes—tricks of scammy manufacturers).

To put it into context, a single pound of saffron takes 75,000 blossoms to produce. Being Iranian, and living among other Iranians in the United States, I had the market for this spice. It's the most expensive legal spice in the world, so it was a great opportunity to make some sales. I did well with it, though it wasn't without its communication challenges. I was selling it to the Iranian diaspora who spoke Farsi, so I had to learn how to interact with my customers who spoke only other languages. There had to be intricacies to my tone. Not only does Farsi itself have different tones from English, but certain tones have different meanings from culture to culture. I also wasn't just speaking to community members, I was speaking to customers. To make each sale, I had to adjust my discourse based on the individual I was speaking to.

Tone is crucial to success in all kinds of communication, including business. Let's explore tone further and see how it can shift based on mood and intention.

HOW TONE, MOOD, AND INTENTION INTERACT

Through the process of starting businesses and working with dozens of partners, freelancers, and mentors, I've had my own troubles with misguided tones. As I touched on in Chapter 2, there were many instances in my life in which what I perceived to be self-confidence worked as the dominant trait in my interactions. However, I think that others saw me as arrogant, and in some cases, I was—because I didn't fully believe in listening to them. I made the mistake of assuming that my point of view was right. With time and a great deal of self-reflection, I learned to stifle my hubris and accept that I had many, many things to learn—and that every interaction I had was a chance to learn more. I learned that I should not only listen better but also change how I conveyed my points of view with the optimal tone for the situation. I learned to create an atmosphere of openness to ensure conversations were heading in the best possible direction. Though this was largely an internal shift in my perspective and mindset, it also had a profound effect on the way in which I interacted with others. Suddenly, my tone became less authoritative and more collaborative. My approach to conversation became more open and understanding. I listened better and I asked for people's opinions because I was more interested in what they had to say and how their experiences could lead me to a greater understanding of the topic at hand.

Tone is absolutely essential because it can be the difference between connection and alienation. Nowhere is this more apparent than at a sports press conference. Here, the tone of questions and answers can shape the whole trajectory of the conversation. Perhaps the best example of this is Allen Iverson's 2002 playoff rant press conference, in which he was asked about missing several practices. The tone of the question seemed to imply that Iverson was lazy. But the reason that Iverson had missed practice was that he was dealing with the loss of his best friend who had died earlier in the season. Iverson responded with a defensive rant that alternated so wildly in tone that it left many in the room speechless.

This press conference would come to be known as the "Practice Rant" because Iverson managed to say the word *practice* in about a dozen different tones.

"PRACTICE?"

"PrAcTicE!"

" . . . *practice* . . ."

He said the word over twenty-two separate times in under four minutes. Deliberately utilizing a variety of tones, Iverson was able to redirect the conversation, moving from an angry basketball player to a humorous critic of the reporters. By changing his tone repeatedly, he made his point while manipulating the situation. Through tone, Iverson was able to deflect the uncomfortable question and make his mark on history at one of the most bizarre sporting press conferences ever. However, he also largely quashed any hope of civil discourse between him and reporters—at that press conference and at many to come.

Naturally, the consequences of that press conference were miniscule, other than Iverson gaining a reputation for being difficult. However, when you look at his mood and tone in relation to discourse in general, it can have a strong impact on the way humans communicate —or fail to communicate—with one another. It shows that mood and intention are interwoven, creating a kind of preparatory mindset that dictates how we convey messages to others, whether that's verbal, written, or in another format entirely.

During the peak breakout of the COVID-19 omicron variant, discourse between vaxxers and anti-vaxxers hit an all-time low. People who wanted to minimize the effects of the virus desperately urged everyone to get vaccinated while anti-vaxxers argued that mandatory vaccinations in workplaces or public spaces infringed on their rights and personal freedoms. As the public so often does during crises, it looked to the leaders of society for guidance. Unfortunately, in the White House's remarkably tone-deaf December 17 written press briefing, President Joe Biden and his administration only fueled the fire by implementing a dark, apocalyptic tone specifically targeting the unvaccinated. One line in particular stood out to many as hostile and unnecessarily grim:

> "For the unvaccinated, you're looking at a
> winter of severe illness and death for yourselves, your
> families, and the hospitals you may soon overwhelm."[7]

Though the White House staffers who ultimately approved this briefing likely had the intention of illustrating the severity of the current situation and the urgency to get vaccinated, they also allowed a certain degree of frustration and hostility to shine through. Naturally, many COVID-19 vaccination advocates and fans of President Biden praised the blunt messaging for calling out those who would put partisan issues and conspiracy theories over the health and safety of their fellow citizens.

Meanwhile, in the minds of anti-vaxxers, the inflammatory briefing further justified the need to stand united against what they viewed as government overreach and antagonism. The tone was accusatory and adopted a fearmongering approach, which led to defensiveness from the anti-vaxxers. It only caused anti-vaxxers to clutch their positions even tighter. The press conference had the opposite effect to what was intended—to use fear to get people vaccinated. For many people caught in the middle, the President failed to instill hope and optimism during a very dark and turbulent time in human history. His tone was likely not successful to his aim—which was to convince the anti-vaxxers and the vaccine-hesitant to get the COVID vaccination.

Consequently, the misguided tone inadvertently worsened public discourse in the middle of a public health crisis. While a more collaborative and understanding tone may not have converted anti-vaxxers, it would not have produced as much ire. A more positive tone wouldn't have riled up those who were already angry about constricting public safety policies.

It is hard to gauge the exact consequences of tone when the discourse is playing out all over the world, but it is far easier to examine the effects of tone on individual discourse. More importantly, it's easier to understand how one can improve tone and use discourse as a way to find a better sense of calm and balance in life.

Tone, Mood, and Intention
QUESTIONS AND ANSWERS

Q: Can I engage in civil discourse if I'm in a bad mood?

A: It is not so much a question of *can* you engage in discourse in a bad mood (some people can), but *should* you? Whether you had a bad day at work or you simply haven't eaten in a while ("hangriness" can be a very destructive force), trying to engage in civil discourse when you are undeniably in a bad mood could muddy your intentions, negatively affect your tone, and make it much harder to keep things civil. So if you are in a bad mood during discourse, you should either disengage until you are ready to return or actively work to recognize and overcome the issue. Oftentimes, just taking a few seconds to close your eyes, breathe, and focus on what you want to achieve can help reduce the negative energy. You can also be upfront with people about already feeling heightened. This allows them to be wary of how it is you are feeling. This can help stop civil discourse from falling apart.

Q: What should I do if someone misinterprets my tone?

A: People misinterpret tone all the time. When this happens, your primary focus should be on clarification and de-escalation. First, clarify what you meant to say and how you meant to convey the information. Then, work to deescalate the situation if someone starts to become angry, emotional, or otherwise negatively affected by their interpretation of your tone. More often than not, you can guide the conversation back to civility through calm explanations and a sincere apology for the misunderstanding. Be sure to regulate your tone (perhaps by making it softer) after it is misinterpreted to ensure that the misunderstanding is less likely to happen again.

Q: How can I use tone to better pursue my intentions?

A: As you will learn in the next section, you have to learn to recognize unique aspects of your tone before you can use it to your (and everyone's) advantage. That said, tone is one of the best ways to maintain the civility that discourse requires should negative emotions arise. Remaining calm, having greater control of yourself, and using a tone that is direct, clear, and collaborative can ensure that you convey your message correctly and pursue your intentions throughout the dialogue.

STUDYING YOUR TONE

As humans, we often like to make everything fit into neat little boxes. Tone is no exception. People will attribute any number of words to describe your tone and view it through their own lens, and perhaps more astute observers may connect it to their understanding of human communication at large. Sometimes, without you realizing it, your tone may sound bitter, angry, optimistic, naive, desperate, reticent, aggressive, ambivalent, indifferent, and so on. While these categorizations might be true to one degree or another, the larger truth is that every single human being has a unique variety of tones. Your unique tone and voice, for that matter, is something that only you possess, and while it may be similar to many others, it is still specific to you.

When I speak about your unique tone, I am using it in practical terms. It comprises multiple facets of your communication style, including:

Your facial :) expressions (including microexpressions!);
Your pacing;
The natural PITCH of your VOICE;
Your "hunched shoulders" body language;
Your language decisions and word choice; and
Even the order in which you use and emphasize words.

As you can see, there are many aspects of tone that you have little power to change.

Take, for instance, the order in which you speak or write words. Word order important incredibly is (sic). It can greatly affect the reaction you get from others, but it is also a reflection of how your brain processes language. Some people have greater control over this aspect of tone than others. One person may struggle to contain "word vomit"—saying things as they come to their mind that are hard to make sense of—while someone else may fill their sentences with pauses and lack confidence by repeating word tics like "um," "ah," and "like." Others may be able to perfectly and eloquently express themselves with few (if any) mistakes and total clarity to multiple listeners. Similarly, someone who is a natural klutz may have less control over their body language, and perhaps it doesn't reflect the words they're saying or the tone they're trying to convey. However, we all have moments when tone has to take over and become our body language, like when we talk over the phone without video. Everyone has a unique way of communicating and therefore has unique tonal strengths, weaknesses, and idiosyncrasies to contend with.

While recognizing broader types of tone in others is relatively easy, it is not always easy to study multifaceted layers of tone in yourself. When you have a conversation with someone, you can usually tell instantaneously what their body language, vocal pitch, and word choice reflect, using broad strokes. Again, you may use words like "aggressive" or "energetic" to describe their tone. However, when analyzing your own tone, you have to try to think not about how *you* perceive your tone but how *others* perceive it.

This brings us back to the always-necessary practice of self-reflection. When you can cultivate a sense of self-awareness that extends beyond your own subjective experience, you have the opportunity to study your behaviors from an objective vantage point. In doing so, you can see how different aspects of your tone affect others, intentionally or unintentionally.

At this point, it is important to emphasize that there is no objectively "correct" tone that one should use during civil discourse. As previously mentioned, while tone is often conflated with vocal pitches and patterns, it extends far beyond that and is wholly unique to each individual. Therefore, it would be impossible (and perhaps counterintuitive) to make everyone conform to a single style of tone. Instead, studying your tone requires you to recognize the unique traits of your natural tone as well as different tones you adopt in different situations.

While there is no way to create an "ideal" tone, there are goals you can pursue when studying and, when necessary, improving your tone for civil discourse. Ultimately, you have to practice discourse to see how people react to your way of communicating. Fortunately, like most people, you've probably spent most of your life interacting, communicating, and observing patterns in the way people react to you. However, you may not have cultivated the self-awareness to detect when it is that your tone causes positive, negative, or even neutral reactions. You may also not have spent much time truly assessing how people respond to you. To ensure you do, make eye contact, watch for body language, and pay attention to others' facial expressions. In paying attention to these reactions, you can deepen your level of awareness. It will help you get better at picking up on individual and human patterns in how your tone tends to come across.

In any case, you should always work to align your tone with your intention during civil discourse. Since your intention should be, generally speaking, finding the truth or reaching mutually beneficial results, this means that your tone should match your intention. If you want to seek out truth, you have to communicate in a way that fosters collaboration between yourself and at least one other party with a shared commitment for uncovering knowledge.

But what does it really mean to have a *collaborative* tone? It's an aspect of collaboration that is easy to identify but difficult to express in detail. When you are taking part in civil discourse, you can feel that your tone is collaborative if it allows the conversation to flow naturally and productively. Even if there are disagreements, misunderstandings, or moments of heated debate, you can trust that your tone is serving your intention if the discourse is moving you closer to truth or mutually beneficial results.

So, to adopt a collaborative tone, you must understand how your way of speaking can contribute to civil discourse. Some people can seem naturally abrasive, condescending, or disagreeable. If you worry that you fall into one of these categories, you will need to work a little harder to cultivate a tone that is more inclusive, calm, and conducive to positive, fruitful discourse. However, everyone has certain strengths and abilities that allow them to communicate effectively. Even if you think that you are terrible at honest communication, if you reflect enough on your behaviors and interactions with others, you are bound to find multiple attributes that can serve you well.

Our digital tone matters, too! One of the greatest challenges I've faced in my first years as a "multipreneur" is helping team members in my companies become aware of their tones when communicating digitally. All my companies are entirely remote, so all tone is filtered through text or computer cameras. Many of us can relate to the tensions that occur when emails or messages don't land with the correct tone, and we often don't think about the tones we use in communication when sifting through huge piles of messages. One downside of these types of messages is that they often linger longer than a spoken statement—which makes tone even more important. Encouraging team members to be patient and open-minded when reading messages or handling long, remote meetings helps diffuse knee-jerk reactions to ambiguous messages. It's important to remember that your digital tone is part of the way you participate in discourse as well.

One way to assess your own digital tone, especially when it comes to written communication, is to read it back to yourself (double points if you read it out loud) and edit it before you click send. There's even software you can use, like Grammarly, that can help detect the tone in your writing. If you're sending an email, it can be beneficial to write a line at the beginning and the end of the email that is friendly in tone. If you, for example, receive a superlong and friendly email and you respond, "Sounds good," you might come across as rude, as if you didn't even read the email. Be especially vigilant with digital communication. Your voice, body language, facial expressions, and other things aren't present to help show your intentions, so you must use language (or maybe even emojis).

Studying Your Tone
QUESTIONS AND ANSWERS

Q: What steps can I take to study my tone?

A: Tone is primarily read through interpretation. This means that in addition to reflecting on the way in which you convey different messages, you also need to pay close

attention to how people react to your words. Since son
people may be more sensitive or apt to misinterpret
words than others, you shouldn't let one reaction out-
weigh the others. Instead, examine your interactions in
general and draw conclusions about how people react
to you more broadly. If others are inclined to engage in
positive dialogues with you, then you are probably utilizing tone to your advantage. Alternatively, if people react
negatively or simply prefer to walk away from discourse
with you, there is almost certainly a tonal issue that you
need to improve.

Plus, don't fall into the trap of assuming that everyone
else is the problem if you notice a pattern of people walking away from you. If you notice a pattern like that, then
examine the constant in this equation—you yourself!

Q: How can I improve my tone?

A: Improving your tone essentially requires you to work on
your communication skills. In my experience, one of the
best ways to improve your tone is listening to successful
communicators and taking note of the different aspects
of their communication styles. Take note of their body
language, their volume, or their word choice.

For example, watching TED Talks can not only help yo
observe collaborative tone in action, but it can also exp
you to new and interesting subjects. It's importa

note that you do not need to mimic other people just to improve your tone, but if you encounter people who know how to communicate effectively and collabora- tively, examine how you can incorporate some aspects of their tone into your own ways of communicating.

Alternatively, you can ask people you know well and trust to give you an honest interpretation of how they perceive your tone. Family, friends, and anyone who is open to giving you an assessment on how you generally carry yourself can be extremely helpful in improving how you conduct civil discourse. After your trusted people let you know, you can also ask them what they think you can do better (and also do a thorough examination on yourself and decide what it is you think will improve your communication).

SUMMARY

Identifying, managing, and even improving tone is one of the most complex elements of civil discourse. Since your tone is a reflec- tion of your personal characteristics, behaviors, and viewpoint, it can feel overwhelming to try to conform to a tone that will be productive in every setting. In fact, it is impossible. After all, the kind of tone that may be conducive to civil discourse with one individual or group may not work as well with another. Therefore, tone—as it relates to discourse—requires you to reflect, self-analyze, listen, and adapt. Remember these points to help you on your journey toward cultivating a more collaborative tone:

- Mood, intent, and tone are all interconnected. However, if your intent is directed toward engaging in civil discourse, you can work to overcome issues with your tone. Just remember that it can be difficult to focus on civil discourse and a collaborative tone when you're in a bad mood!

- Everyone's tone is unique, and you shouldn't feel bad if your tone is misinterpreted. Instead, focus on the strengths and weaknesses of your own communication skills and address any misunderstandings promptly.

- Study your tone through self-reflection and observation of people's reactions. You will almost always find that there are ways that you can better communicate ideas with your tone. You'll improve civil discourse in the process.

FINAL QUESTIONS AND ANSWERS

Q: What should I do if people refuse to use a collaborative tone with me?

A: Like with civil discourse in general, you can't force anyone to play nice. Even if you have cultivated a collaborative tone, you may still experience resistance, perhaps even aggression. In these kinds of situations, civil discourse is much harder to achieve. However, using a calm, collaborative tone is kind of like smiling or laughing—it tends to be infectious. When you encounter unproductive tones, double down on your desire to collaborate. More often than not, this will make it very difficult for others to resist the urge to engage in truly civil discourse.

Chapter Four
Trust

Let's discuss going into business with Sheldon the turtle.

At thirteen, I was pretty young to be a turtle breeder. I couldn't rely on being an established adult that other turtle sellers might have been more likely to engage with. That was why I had to build a strong sense of trust between myself and the people I was selling to. I wasn't automatically a name people were familiar with.

When you hear the name *Martha Stewart*, you think about home goods. When you hear *Apple*, you think about phones and computers. People buy things from these brands because the name *itself* communicates quality home goods, recipes, or electronics. When you hear *Milan Kordestani*, though, you probably don't think about turtles. Perhaps you don't think anything at all!

That's why I had to be so careful with my words. When I communicated with a potential buyer, it was crucial that I demonstrated I knew what I was talking about and spoke with a calm confidence that made me—at least in a business sense—come across as more mature. I couldn't rely on a name or a brand. But also, because the people I interacted with couldn't know me or see me, they had to have a large degree of faith—faith in my knowledge, savviness, or general business sense.

I'm not the first person to step into business while trying to find their footing at a young age. Many before me also required trust from others to believe that they were ready and needed self-conviction to know that they could achieve their goals.

Oprah Winfrey, the popular and wildly successful TV host, knows a thing or two about trust. She never could have built the global audience that she did if her audience didn't trust her to be vulnerable, to be honest, and to tackle even the most controversial topics with fairness and thought.

Oprah Winfrey's success as a talk show host illustrates the essential role trust and faith play in civil discourse. Despite facing consistent discrimination as a Black woman in the entertainment industry, viewers had to develop faith in Oprah's ability to maintain civility in the pursuit of common ground, even in the most challenging and sensitive of conversations. Her big break came in 1986 with the launch of her own show, *The Oprah Winfrey Show*, which attracted huge numbers: 40 million weekly viewers tuning in from across 150 countries.

Oprah's self-confidence and belief in her own capabilities as a host were key to her success. She was able to navigate difficult conversations with bad-faith actors, even if she did not align with them at first. Oprah's grace and poise in each of those instances allowed her to push boundaries in the entertainment industry by taking risks others would not feel comfortable taking. Her unwavering faith in herself to lead any conversation to a positive learning outcome led to a lasting impact on the lives of generations of Americans, such as myself and my mother. Oprah's story emphasizes that trust and faith in oneself and others is crucial for advancing civil discourse and inspiring positive societal change.

But Oprah, like any of us trying to engage in discourse, didn't always get it right. In 1988, Oprah interviewed a gang of skinheads who argued that White people were responsible for creating everything in the United States. Reflecting back on it, she said that the interview was so tense that she felt like she was on "volatile ground." She realized that she'd made a mistake by having them on the show and that she no longer wanted to feel that energy in the room or bring that energy to people again. She made the decision to never let her platform—with a reach of millions—be a forum for people attempting to spread hate. While she'd had faith that she could have a discourse, she was not able to build trust with them. Sometimes, that's how it ends up in a conversation.

Oprah didn't lose viewers after that incident. In fact, her viewership only grew. When we trust someone, we don't unthinkingly trust them to always do the right thing. We trust them to act in good faith, to recognize when change is necessary, and to act on that change. And, ultimately, the skinheads she had on her show returned to apologize.

Oprah has proven herself by bringing a level of spiritual and thoughtful discourse into everything she does. In a speech given to graduates at Colorado College in 2019, one year before I graduated, she opened with a quote from Angela Davis: "You have to act as if it's possible to radically transform the world and you have to do that all the time."[8]

She later went on to say that everyone has a chance to change the world every day, through every small step—one "life-transforming" step at a time. She preaches that each of us should work to find a solution. To find a solution to the world's problems, you have to trust yourself and trust others to help turn this quest into reality.

Oprah believes that life is all about every decision you make over time. It's all about being of service to others, using kindness as much as possible, and acting to "radically transform any moment you're in." In terms of my own growth, I owe a lot to Oprah. She helped me realize the importance of mantras to help me get through life. During the speech at Colorado College, she got people to repeat, multiple times, the following mantra: "Everything is always working out for me." She then told everyone to take the mantra and "make it yours." These mantras help people have faith in themselves—faith that opens one up to trust.

I want to explore the separate but interrelated concepts of faith and trust. Without them, civil discourse simply cannot happen. Thus, it's vital to understand how to cultivate these skills first in yourself and then in others, like Oprah did to maximize her career and life. We'll examine the importance of trusting the process of civil discourse and having faith in its outcomes. This begins by nurturing your sense of self-trust and cultivating others' trust in you and your vision.

TRUST AND FAITH

Without some degree of faith, civil discourse cannot exist. Every participant must decide to enter the conversation with sincere intention(s). More specifically, they must desire to find the truth or bring about mutually beneficial results for all parties. While trust is generally regarded as something that must be cultivated over time, you must show a willingness to have faith in others to engage in civil discourse—whether or not you truly know their intentions.

Faith is a necessary building block of civil discourse. At its most basic form, faith is merely the act of believing in something without the need for proof or evidence. It doesn't always need to be profound or cosmic. You can have faith that your house will protect you from the elements, that your alarm will wake you up on time, or that your steps won't collapse when you go upstairs. However, when you extend your faith to other human beings, it takes on greater significance. Having faith in someone else, especially someone you have never met before, takes a great degree of courage. If you believe that humans are capable of good and that most (or at least some) people are well-intentioned, you can equip yourself to extend faith to others.

So how does trust come into play? In a sense, trust is simply a stronger, more grounded version of faith. If having faith is to believe in something without proof or evidence, trust is to believe in something based on existing evidence. When the Wright brothers first began their experiments with aviation at the turn of the century, they had faith in their ability to get a heavier-than-air "flying machine" off the ground. Many thought this feat would be impossible and that gravity was a force too strong for humans to counteract and overcome. However, after extensive research and flight tests, the brothers went deeper into their ambitions. They designed a moveable rudder to allow for greater control in the air.

Their hard work and the vast body of evidence they amassed proved their idea's workability and transformed the faith they had in themselves into trust. Thus, on December 17, 1903, the two brothers succeeded in creating the first controlled flight of a power-driven airplane. Now billions of people trust the Wright brothers' invention enough to fly every year, and technology has increased in sophistication, allowing us to put people in space and on the moon. How long until we're landing on Mars and beyond?

We often think about the concept of trust as something we should only share with a select group of people. We trust our family, our close friends, and our employees. We also trust bus drivers, servers, and cashiers to carry out various functions under their respective institutions. However, outside this functional paradigm, when someone new enters our personal orbit, we tend to withhold trust until they have "earned" it. While this may help us avoid certain situations or relationships that don't serve our best interests, it also prevents us from openly and honestly engaging in tens, if not hundreds, of meaningful conversations.

Of course, one should always practice a degree of caution when extending trust to others. I'm not saying you should trust everyone you meet without exception or reservation. Sometimes, your intuition tells you not to trust someone—and you tend to feel this in the pit of your stomach. Although this bodily reaction can misfire, it often turns out to be correct. Your body has an intelligence in and of itself that sometimes feels separate from the brain, a natural instinct to know who to trust.

However, in most cases, I firmly believe in giving people the benefit of the doubt. We should trust someone unless they break that trust rather than not trust someone until they earn it. To cultivate this trust in others, faith can serve you well. Faith allows you to give people a chance to prove their sincerity. A strong sense of trust takes time and effort to develop, and faith is the precursor that allows trust to flourish. However, a basic sense of faith and a temporary delay of suspicion is instantaneous—*just add water!* Both of these actions are necessary for open conversations. So, while trust requires time, effort, and a great deal of evidence to cultivate, faith involves none of these. You can simply have faith in someone and, if proven correct over time, build that faith into the strong bond that is trust.

TRUSTING THE PROCESS OF CIVIL DISCOURSE

Let's dig further into applying the issue of trust in order to open the lanes of dialogue and discussion. While trust is a valuable quality for its own sake, it is also a necessary ingredient for civil discourse. Therefore, you must have faith in the process that trust will build over time. The more you cultivate this civility, the more you will help society cultivate it, too.

But herein lies the essential problem: it can be difficult to have faith that civil discourse is possible. But it is possible, and when it's in full flow, it thrives. Therefore, I'm encouraging you to take the leap of faith and, if you don't already, start to believe that civil discourse is possible.

However, I do understand that at the macro-level, it's often rather challenging to believe in civil discourse. It's especially difficult in the United States to have faith and goodwill for those we don't know beyond the surface level. We live in a moment of time when pride in the United States is dangerously low and political strife and partisanship seem to be either pushing people to the extremes of the political spectrum or simply burning them out so much that they no longer care. It seems that most people are either politically intense or politically apathetic with no in-between. Those who are politically intense shout the loudest, are heard the most on social media platforms or newsrooms, and can make us feel that they represent the majority of the "opposite view." Those who are apathetic may be so in fear of voicing their opinions because a mob of people (often digital, but also in the tangible world) will shout them down until they decide to move on to the next victim.

One of the problems with civil discourse in its current dire situation is the assumption that it will sort itself out over time. If it will just sort itself out, what's the point in putting any effort into fixing it? You may have felt a similar sense of apathy at different levels. Whether it involves a lack of knowing or caring for your neighbor, seeing a homeless person on the street and wondering why someone else won't fix the "problem," or just going about your daily life thinking that the issue is everyone around you. Wouldn't everything be better if people just thought more like you? With this mindset, the many problems our world faces will only get worse.

If you're asking yourself questions like "How could I possibly have faith or trust in the people who don't share the same values as me?" just know that you don't need to share the same values to make progress between two people or groups with opposing views. In fact, there may be many cases where you identify the same problem as someone who you consider your opposite, but perhaps you disagree on the *solution* to the problem. There may even be cases when you share a consensus about how to solve an issue. In the pursuit of common ground between two groups with adversarial values, we know that civil discourse can lead to progress and a "win-win" for all parties involved. It is possible to recognize the value or basis of someone's opinions without necessarily compromising on your own. Whether it's two siblings coming to an agreement about whose turn it is to sit in the front seat or nations with different political ideologies learning to collaborate on global initiatives, this sort of collaboration can lead to real solutions.

For all the benefits the Internet and digital connectivity has provided us, when we connect ourselves to all others around the world at all hours of the day with instant access to everything from news reports, cat videos, and every single opinion imaginable, we glut ourselves into malaise and work ourselves up into malice. Next time you're walking down the street, look around you. How many people's necks are bent over with blue light bouncing off their semi-grinning, zombified faces? I don't know anyone who hasn't been guilty of this. We're losing out on valuable eye contact and human-to-human inter-action. What is this lack of genuine connectivity—the connections formed, not through fiber optics, but through the fibers of our very nature—doing to us?

As the skill to make new *real-life* friends dissipates, finding com-mon ground becomes more difficult. Conducting civil discourse becomes harder because it means we lack the constant reminders of "good" that re-instill our faith and trust in people who are not next to us. We are only walking in circles in our shared echo chambers. When it's harder to create thirty-second relationships with people around us—ones that open new social pathways to people who were previously complete strangers—we inherently become more anxious and closed off as human beings.

Furthermore, our behaviors are turning us into tech-addled addicts. We wear headphones through the airport and on the plane. We stare at our phones in elevators and allow notifications to pop-off in our pockets every twenty seconds. We speak straight into headsets as we press buttons on a controller or keyboard to take headshots rather than get out there and make lasting relationships in the real world. These are just some of the effects of a technological addiction, with the symptoms being decreased empathy, increased isolation, and even back and neck problems due to poor posture. While it's evident throughout the whole population, it's especially disturbing to see this affliction manifesting in adolescents and younger people.

In fact, according to research conducted by Asurion, Americans check their phones ninety-six times a day.[9] That is a shocking statistic that shows how much we have our heads elsewhere: inside our machines.

The avoidant behavior we see and experience as a result of having smartphones and being constantly "plugged in" has deep ramifications for how we interact in the real world. We use technology in place of boredom or uncomfortability. It cuts into our daily life and makes us less resilient to awkwardness or disagreement. It makes us more fragile when we are confronted with some of life's more pressing issues. Instead of engaging with those different from us, we opt to speak to people who will parrot what we already believe. If we anticipate awkwardness we may therefore stop ourselves from engaging in civil discourse, which will inevitably stop personal growth and bring society's overall progression to a screeching halt.

For most, the loss of the ability to conduct civil discourse was slow, recent, and didn't happen overnight. For others, civil discourse was never even a reality. These people may have been born into a belief system of assumptions and biases about anyone their upbringing taught them was the "other." In either case, the assumptions of a bad experience keep us as individuals from interacting with the perceived other and, unfortunately, keep us from growing or progressing as a society. After all, strong societies are built on trust. Think about it. You're never going to get a loan from a bank if they don't trust you'll pay it back. You'd also never put money in a bank if you didn't trust you'd be able to spend your own money. You'd never order takeout if you didn't trust you'd get your food. When we assume awkwardness, opposition, laziness, or someone's attitude is going to be combative, we lose the opportunity for civil discourse before it even begins.

You must have trust that you are capable of conducting civil discourse, rebuild the skill of creating a thirty-second relationship, and find common ground with anyone who thinks differently than you. For example, you will find a near-unanimous agreement upon the statement "family is essential," regardless of political ideology or personal background. We'll discuss finding common ground further in Chapter 8. For now, just know that civil discourse can spring from a place of agreement before it pulls into other, more nuanced areas.

While we know that not everyone in this world is interested in civil discourse, we have to have trust in our own abilities and skills to manipulate discourse to consistently be in search of what unites us. Start by making every conversation a version of "closing the deal." It's like being a used car salesman, but what you're selling is not a point, it's common ground. It goes further than that, though. Have faith that anyone you encounter—be it a waiter, coworker, or family doctor—is an opportunity for you to practice trust in yourself and faith in others. By conducting civil discourse with someone who you'll have to have faith in, you will be able to grow as a person who's well-intentioned. You'll find that negative interactions don't last long or might not even happen at all, as most people want positive interactions that can help their days be filled with positivity.

While negative interactions will inevitably happen from time to time, you need to trust that you did your utmost to conduct civil discourse and that your faith in humanity—though maybe challenged in that moment—should remain strong. If something *is* uncivil, you can remind yourself that we are all human (and prone to a vast, ever-shifting spectrum of emotions). Sometimes, you may speak to someone on an off day, which makes them respond with more shortness or more frustration than before. Just because you have one more uncivil interaction with someone, it doesn't mean that your interactions with them are a fixed pattern. We all have the ability to change and become better, more gentle conversationalists.

Though civil discourse may be especially challenging to facilitate during fractured times, the process itself has stood the test of time for centuries. It is possible to get us back to that method of communication. If you fail to trust civil discourse because you think that people are too closed-minded to engage in the practice, you're only adding to the problem. Instead, trust in the process, and allow yourself to believe that civil discourse not only works but that it is crucial to the progress of society. In doing so, you can engage in the practice yourself and help others do the same. I'm not asking you to believe in some kind of strict dogma without any grounding in reality. History has proven that civil discourse exists, it works, and—with the support and trust of enough people—it can work again. The first revolution is within, and like a pebble dropped into a lake, once we help facilitate civil discourse, our actions will ripple outward onto others.

Trust and Faith
QUESTIONS AND ANSWERS

Q: To me, faith implies religion, and I am not religious. How does this apply to me?

A: Faith is a belief in something with limited or no evidence. Yes, people who are religious have faith and believe in things they cannot see, but they are not the only ones who have faith. We may have faith that politicians will act in our best interests. We have faith that our favorite artist's next album will be worth listening to. We have faith in our sports teams, our soldiers, and our loved ones. Some of this is trust, but that's what stems from the seed of faith. In many ways, faith is what ties us together. It gives us something we can feel hopeful about. Therefore, faith is something we all need in some way.

Q: If someone has burned me in the past, how do I know it is safe to trust them again?

A: Distrusting someone does not fully impede productive dialogue. What matters is that you trust the process of civil discourse. If you're overly concerned about the intentions of someone who has taken advantage of your trust in the past, you won't be able to focus on creating an environment in which you can both move forward. Therefore, you should try to leave the past in the past.

That said, you should never completely forget when someone has a history of lying or cheating to "win" an argument. If the person demonstrates a certain pattern of behavior, it's a good thing to be at least somewhat wary. This will help you better understand how to manage the conversation. However, don't allow a lack of trust to stand in the way of discourse. Instead, use it to understand the other person and their perspective better.

Finally, it is possible someone is simply behaving as a bad-faith actor—check out Chapter 10, "Avoiding Poor Discourse," to learn how to handle discourse with "trolls."

ONE STEP BACK, TWO STEPS FORWARD

Trust is something that you must also have in yourself. Just like having faith in yourself, self-trust comes from prolonged and sincere introspection. Self-trust is often confused with self-confidence. Though the two concepts are related, they differ in one important way. Self-confidence reflects the faith you have in yourself, but it is often displayed as a projection to others. You can be dubbed "self-confident" if you display the right attitude and quality of confidence. However, self-trust is a mostly internal action. Self-confidence can be a façade for the public, but self-trust cannot. Self-trust must be genuine. The difference may seem like mere semantics, but it's vital for the sake of entering discourse in earnest.

To trust yourself, you must take inventory of your abilities. You must make a conscious effort to recognize and understand your strengths, weaknesses, limitations, and biases. In short, you must practice self-reflection, which is how you bypass the protective nature of your ego and understand who you want to be and who you currently are. This is accomplished through a dialogue with your inner self. It will allow you to be yourself and live as genuinely as possible. When you can live authentically, you have nothing to hide and therefore have little, if any, justification for distrusting yourself.

Self-knowlege intimately removes the need to withhold trust on the grounds of ignorance. Once you spot, for instance, certain destructive behaviors, treat them with reverence and listen to why you carry out these behaviors. Then, you can dismantle them and put new ones in their places. Essentially, you can have a civil discourse and understand yourself better, bringing about more positive and constructive days.

When early humans first encountered one another on the African continent, they likely distrusted one another because they did not *know* one another. Distrust can be a useful survival technique. It serves a protective function. However, when you truly know yourself, you take away the primary reason you have to distrust yourself. If you know who you are and see yourself realistically, you can be trusted to act in line with your deepest intentions. We've all had that moment when we're deciding between getting up and going for a run or sitting on the sofa and eating potato chips. If you trust yourself to act in line with your inner self, you will be able to operate more effectively in the world and, as a bonus, have a better time doing it.

Once you come to know yourself, you must accept your limitations without succumbing to them—awareness is the first step. If you're having a conversation, for example, and you feel out of your depth, that's okay. You can admit that and move forward, which can help the person you're talking with trust you even more. When you accept your limitations, you can give yourself greater confidence to maintain civility during discourse—rather than just thinking you're always right and the person you're talking to is clearly wrong for having an alternative viewpoint.

But what exactly does civility in discourse mean? It means that you must know what you can and can't do, but that doesn't mean you should underestimate yourself. Every day is a new day for growth—a day for us to further cultivate our strengths and help improve our weaknesses. You can get better every day. It is not always easy to maintain civility because it requires a deep understanding of your abilities, goals, and all the tools and resources at your disposal. You must know the limits of your understanding when engaging in civil discourse, but you must also believe in your own knowledge and skills so that you can engage others confidently and courteously. You can approach others and listen to them but also trust what comes out of your mouth. In my experience, there are often times when someone goes to silence themselves after they seem like they're going to throw an idea or thought into the conversational mix. Ironically, when someone silences themselves and I pry them to go further, that is often when they say the most deeply insightful things.

Countless examples of trusting one's speech can be drawn from the world of professional writing where many of the industry's greatest success stories are flush with setbacks, hurdles, and determination. Let's look at some examples.

Stephen King is the horror genre equivalent of Dickens or Shakespeare, but when he was a new writer, publishers rejected his first work over thirty times. Today, his novel *Carrie* is hailed as one of the greatest works of twentieth-century horror. But King famously explained, "By the time I was fourteen, the nail in my wall would no longer support the weight of the rejection slips impaled upon it. I replaced the nail with a spike and went on writing."[10] This is the mantra of an artist whose self-trust is strong. King recognized his limitations as a writer and a storyteller, but he also knew his strengths. Despite failing time and time again, he had trust in himself and faith that a publisher would see the value in his work. Fortunately, his wife believed in him, too, and she encouraged him to pick himself up and try again and again until he got it right.

We should approach self-trust like King. Of course, I'm sure moments of doubt have had him questioning his own abilities. But he persisted. He trusted himself enough to keep writing, keep sending to publishers, and keep refining his craft. Now he's a household name. We must all find a way to trust ourselves—especially when it comes to our own words, ideas, and ability to communicate—to ensure we move society forward. We must take note of our limitations but also look beyond them to see what is still on the horizon. After being rejected dozens of times, King could have given up. Even at the time, people must have argued that he could have, or perhaps even should have, thrown in the towel. Thankfully, he had enough self-belief, faith, and trust to persevere, becoming one of the greatest and most famous storytellers of his generation.

To trust yourself, you must know yourself and know what you want to do. This can be interpreted at both a micro and macro scale. If you want to engage in civil discourse, you should understand yourself through self-reflection and enter the conversation to find truth or produce mutually beneficial results.

One Step Back, Two Steps Forward
QUESTIONS AND ANSWERS

Q: What kinds of activities can I do to build my self-trust?

A: We should all try, every day, to challenge ourselves in new ways so that we can build self-trust. One of the best ways to build your self-trust through new challenges is by succeeding at hobbies and being part of a community that embraces those hobbies. This means that no matter what you enjoy or want to learn, any kind of activity can build self-trust.

For example, embrace learning a new artistic hobby: woodworking, baking, DJing, photography, poetry, making hats for rubber ducks—the options are endless. Each time you create something original (and thus beautiful), you gain trust in your own abilities, as well as your ability to connect with others and share a vision. By proactively challenging yourself, you gain self-trust and the confidence to communicate with people around you.

There are many ways to take on new challenges in your hobby; from working out harder to see results, to learning to paint and loving your work, to getting the little hats to be just the right size to fit your bath toys. Challenges like these are great ways to learn more about yourself and learn to trust yourself. Ultimately, it's about creating a mindset where you know you can succeed so that you are more confident in facing new challenges.

Q: How do I change my mindset toward one of self-trust?

A: Self-reflection is a great way to increase your self-trust. Think about successes and failures in your past. Think about how those successes were achieved and what you learned from the failures. Focus on the lessons you learned, but also think about how you are deserving of that self-trust. If you have trouble being honest with yourself, use self-reflection as a tool to evaluate your self-deceit. Why do you struggle to tell yourself the truth and, in turn, struggle to trust yourself? The more you practice self-reflection and ask these kinds of questions, the more your self-confidence and self-trust will flourish!

TRUSTING OTHERS

Trust doesn't exist in a vacuum. If you trust yourself, you must also be able to trust others. If the only person you trust is you, then you are going to have a hard time engaging in civil discourse. In fact, you should trust yourself enough to trust others, but you must also be trustworthy to others so that *they* trust *you* in turn.

Trust is something you must also have in your team and your vision. Just like having faith in yourself, self-trust comes from prolonged and sincere introspection. Henry Ford famously doubled the wages of his assembly-line employees to $5 per day despite declining car sales at the time. This was twice the national average income in 1914. By increasing the salaries of his workforce, he created a whole new group of potential car buyers. His workers could afford to buy the cars they were making, giving a much-needed boost to sales while significantly reducing worker turnover.[11] He trusted his instincts, and it paid dividends.

Self-trust is an essential quality in entrepreneurs like Ford, but it also reflects a kind of universal faith in humanity. Ford believed in his vision, which was highly unorthodox among the early twentieth century's business elite. Some people around him, including other entrepreneurs, doubted his ideas. This sort of environment makes self-trust even more important. Although it's essential to hear out what other people have to say about your ideas, at the end of the day, your self-trust can override other people's doubts. Ultimately, Ford thought that both his workers and the general public would respond positively to his ideas, and they did. By having both faith and trust in himself, Ford also had to put a great deal of faith in the men and women of his day, which helped him easily drive past the competition.

Doubling the salaries of his workers could have spelled financial ruin for the Ford Motor Company. After all, sales were down, and the market of people who could afford his cars was still relatively small. So Ford put his faith in people and trust in his product. He believed that with better salaries, his workers would want to buy Ford cars—and he was 100 percent correct. As a result, increasing his workers' salaries gained their trust. Over time, Ford built mutual trust between himself and his workers, which made his workforce far more loyal to the Ford brand in the process.

Any good leader uses trust to not just succeed for themselves but for the good of all those who they are responsible for. When you think of a civil rights leader, who comes to mind? Maybe Martin Luther King or Nelson Mandela or Harriet Tubman. What made these people successful? They proved to those they led that they believed in their cause. Martin Luther King, for example, didn't just tell others what to do. He practiced what he preached by engaging in sit-ins and marching in the streets. He showed others in the fight that he was willing to get arrested for what he believed in. That's how you build trust. You prove that you mean what you say.

The lesson here is about *transparency*. Not everyone has a team of people on an assembly line building their car or an entire movement ready to march across the bridge with them. But most people have a community of some sort. It could be a group of friends, it could be your family, children, your coworkers, or a combination of all of them. A lot of us carry the heavy weight of our egos and pride around, using that as a barometer to help us decide who we want to be, who we think we are, and what we believe other people think of us. Our egos, however, aren't great guides when it comes to cultivating a personality. Our egos are only really helpful for survival. If you constantly act from a place of ego-consciousness, always chasing the next big thing without being relatable to most people, you'll find it difficult to be transparent. Instead, we must look within and listen to the quieter inner voice (our conscience) to ensure we act in ways that are true to ourselves.

Part of the challenge in trusting yourself when conducting civil discourse is that you need to trust yourself to occasionally make judgment calls around when you disclose opinions, share vulnerabilities, or push the boundaries of what's generally considered "appropriate" in order to close the distance between people. Trust is most often built through transparency. When others trust that your intentions are civil, then you will be able to close the relationship gap and find common ground. You can do this even when it's clear you may have competing perspectives. Transparency is how others find perspectives rather than be enclosed in an echo chamber.

In both work and my personal life, I'm often known to break the "fourth wall" in conversations. This means that when a conversation begins to get uncivil, I will generally call it out in a very intentional way, to bring everyone's individual attention back to the way in which they're delivering their words. I challenge the delivery rather than the opinions themselves.

These examples demonstrate a great advantage to be gained in business when workers and employers have faith in each other and support each other in a mutually beneficial way. It can and should be extrapolated far beyond CEOs and paychecks, however. By adding positivity into the lives of those around us while asking them to trust our visions and ideas, we can build an ever-growing circle of people to engage with for civil discourse. If we want others to believe in our vision, we have to show them where they fit into it. We need them to trust that we know how they can also be a part of it all.

Faith in Others
QUESTIONS AND ANSWERS

Q: I'm somewhat wary of strangers. How can I grow my faith in them more quickly so that I can have civil and meaningful discourse with them?

A: You must recognize that you only need a small amount of faith in the other to begin civil discourse. Have faith that a stranger is coming to you with respectful intentions. If you're wrong, disengage as needed, but as civil discourse grows, support and nurture it. Then, as you successfully engage in civil discourse, you will naturally develop faith in those strangers.

Half the battle is ensuring that you bring civil discourse to the table. You don't have to trust a stranger completely to engage with them. You only need to have faith in humanity's ability to use civil discourse for good. This will provide you with just enough faith in strangers to enter an open and honest dialogue.

Q: How can I increase others' trust in me and my vision?

A: It may be a cliché, but because it rings true, it's worth repeating: honesty really is the best policy. When you have a history of being honest and forthright with people, they are far more likely to take you at your word and believe in your vision. This is another reason why lying and manipulation are antithetical to productive discourse. They erode trust and make it much harder for others to willingly listen to what you have to say.

SUMMARY

In this chapter, we've explored the separate but interrelated concepts of faith and trust and discussed how to better integrate these ideas into our lives to promote civil discourse. It is vital to cultivate faith and trust in yourself and others. Once you do, you can approach civil discourse with good intentions, an openness to listen to others, and the ability to converse respectfully.

Remember these points to ensure you maximize the usefulness of trust in your life and conversations.

- Faith means believing in something without the need for proof or evidence. Alternatively, trust means believing in something based on existing evidence. Both are an essential part of civil discourse: having faith in the process and your discussion and trust in yourself.

- While it's easy to look at social media and feel like civil discourse is impossible, trust the process. Civil discourse is possible, and we don't even have to have faith—there's lots of evidence to demonstrate that humans have an ability to let civil discourse thrive.

- Self-trust is the core of maintaining respect during open conversations. Cultivate self-trust by knowing yourself, reflecting on your abilities and limits, and accepting limitations without succumbing to them.

- Reward others when they achieve, and show them you are trustworthy by trusting in them. The best discourse occurs when both sides have demonstrated that they trust each other. This leads to both of them working together for that mutually beneficial result.

- Remember that the other person in the discussion is not an opponent but a peer seeking mutual benefit and understanding. Have faith in that relationship and that other person, and do not treat them poorly—common ground is the best location for civil discourse.

FINAL QUESTIONS AND ANSWERS

Q: What about "imposter syndrome"? Doesn't that affect our ability to trust ourselves, and affect how we interact with others?

A: First of all, imposter syndrome is absolutely real, and everyone, even the most influential CEOs or most talented artists struggle with it from time to time. Imposter syndrome is a lack of self-trust: a feeling that you are a hidden imposter not qualified to do your job or talented enough to succeed. Imposter syndrome may leave you feeling unsure of yourself or even defensive when critiqued, and that can be a roadblock to civil discourse. But it's also important to remember that everyone has the experience of imposter syndrome; we should empathize with others and be patient with ourselves. Ultimately, trust in your own abilities and trust that others are confident in you as well. Your feeling of being an imposter will pass, and you'll be confident in any conversation you approach.

Q: How do we handle discourse with someone we cannot trust?

A: When you're in a discourse with someone who you cannot trust, you shouldn't anticipate a sudden change of heart. This isn't to say that you should write off everything as a lie. However, you cannot simply believe everything someone tells you, especially if that person has proven themselves to be untrustworthy.

So what does discourse with an untrustworthy person look like? In the most basic terms, it is a dialogue in which you must consistently steer the conversation back toward truth. If the person tells a lie—or something that could be a lie—counter it with the truth. Don't make accusations or feel angry that you've been lied to. Simply say what you know to be accurate and allow the process of civil discourse to play out.

Part II

In Practice

Chapter Five
Active Listening

My parents' divorce hurt me deeply, and it happened, in part, because of a breakdown in civil discourse in their relationship. Their divorce was a turning point in my life. Growing up with my parents together, it seemed inevitable that they would stay together for the rest of their lives. Our family unit was unbreakable, right? When I was nine, however, they informed my sister and me that they were separating. As you'd probably expect, this was painful. As a kid, adults tend to force you to apologize and reconcile differences with each other, so perhaps my naivete left me confused as to why common ground could not be found more easily between a married couple—especially my parents. However, I learned the hard way how easy it is for communication to fail. And many marriages fall apart due to a breakdown in effective, open, and honest communication. Compounded with this was the sense of isolation I felt when my parents both, separately, moved us to England that same year, where I was the Brown kid at the predominantly White school.

Having spent a significant portion of my life with divorced parents, I often look at the high divorce rates and wonder why so many couples end up going their separate ways. When you look at court documents, the vast majority of divorces are attributed to "irreconcilable differences." While the breakdown of marriages and other romantic relationships is far too complex to attribute to one single factor, irreconcilable differences is a broad, catch-all term that really gets to the heart of divorce. Couples reach impasses, and for one reason or another, they cannot find a way forward that allows them to continue being married.

The truth is that few differences are completely irreconcilable, yet roughly a quarter of American marriages end in divorce.[12] That's not as high as the common misconception that says half of all marriages don't work out, but it's still quite a lot. So why do so many marriages end? Because, more often than not, at least one person fails to communicate their wants, needs, and goals effectively to their significant other. You may be reading this and think that the responsibility falls on the person attempting to communicate their wants, needs, and goals, but that is only half of the process of communicating. Someone may be a terrible communicator, or they may be the best communicator possible, but either way, most discussions break down because one or both parties are not *listening*.

Doubt me that listening is crucial to a long-lasting marriage? Well, the animal with the best hearing in the world is the greater wax moth. Have you ever heard of a greater wax moth getting divorced?

Communication breakdowns can often lead to resentment, a huge divorce predictor. If someone stays silent about an aspect of their other half's behavior, but their other half is totally unaware of their own behavior, it's extremely unlikely anything will improve. The feeling of resentment can then snowball from there. What I've noticed is that addressing issues as soon as they arise and openly discussing things that are affecting the relationship—and each party committing to better themselves—can lead to a much happier marriage and significantly reduce the chances of divorce. In short, it's easy to hear, but it's more of a challenge to listen.

ACTIVE LISTENING VERSUS PASSIVE LISTENING

In Chapters 3 and 4, I briefly touched on the importance of *listening*. It is one thing to hear what someone is saying, but to really understand their intention and tone, you have to practice active listening—like our good friend Mr. Rogers. Active listening is truly listening. It's letting someone else talk and fully interacting with what they're saying, even paraphrasing it back so that they can say whether you understand them correctly. These are just some of the ways to achieve this.

The problem is that some people are better at active listening than others. It doesn't mean you are a bad person if you have trouble listening to others; it could simply be a result of your culture, upbringing, values, or even your brain chemistry. Consequently, some people have to work much harder to be active listeners during civil discourse or a general conversation. But active listening is also a practiced skill, which means everyone has the capacity to improve their active listening skills, no matter what their unpracticed capability is.

So what does it mean to be an active listener? It's actually very simple. An active listener hears and understands messages as they are intended to be perceived by the speaker. In other words, rather than using your own biases, assumptions, and knee-jerk reactions to interpret what someone is saying, you must work to adopt their point of view as you listen. It means understanding how to read the messages implied by the speaker without attributing any additional intentionality to that speaker. In that sense, it's a complex skill that requires discipline. It means avoiding the pitfalls of bias as much as possible. However, before you can become an active listener, you must first cultivate the ability to listen for basic comprehension.

Have you ever found your mind wandering aimlessly while someone else is speaking? Maybe your dad was telling you about his day and you started thinking about something more interesting, like the invention of the envelope. Your mind sometimes jumps to a task you need to complete that day, or maybe even what you will say next. Or have you ever asked a question, only to have your brain zone out when the other person gives you the answer? If so, you're not alone. Many people struggle to listen for comprehension. It even shows up in the classroom. Some students are classified as visual learners or tactile learners. Both kinds of learners absorb information better when they are not required to listen as much. It's not a fault or a shortcoming; it's more that there are multiple ways for a brain to process information successfully, and human diversity means that not all our brains operate the same way (because how boring would that be?!).

Assuming that you do struggle with listening, even if just on rare occasions, it's best to practice good listening habits for the future.

Here are a few strategies that have helped me immensely with my basic listening comprehension in a wide range of environments:

1. Make an extra effort to keep your brain focused on the conversation. This may require you to block out both external and internal distractions. Additionally, letting the other person know that you are listening can help improve discourse. You can do this by nodding, making eye contact, using open body language (no crossed arms), and saying things like "mhmm" or "oh!" to demonstrate that you are actively engaged in the discussion.

2. Repeat some or all of what someone says back to them— but paraphrase it to show you understand and are not just parroting. Use short statements that hold greater value or importance in the conversation. Often, saying words aloud—"Yes, radishes!" or "Rubber bands, really?"—will help you understand them better and ensure that you don't miss out on any pertinent information. It also reassures the speaker that you've been listening, which increases their confidence in the conversation.

3. If you prefer not to say the words aloud, repeat what someone says in your head before responding or even considering a response. *Grandma's favorite food is radishes,* or *All of the rubber bands have gone missing.* Much like saying the words aloud, this will allow you to ruminate on what the speaker communicated. This technique will also help with information recall later, should you revisit the discussion.

4. Pay attention to tone and body language as these can be just as important as the content of a conversation. In fact,

they can put the words in a context that you might have otherwise overlooked.

5. Ask questions to improve clarity. This doesn't mean that you should just ask inane questions to give the impression that you are engaged in the conversation—like "Do you know any good recipes that use radishes?" or "Do you remember when we made that huge ball of rubber bands?" Rather, ask questions to help you better understand an alternative perspective—like "Isn't your grandpa allergic to radishes, though?" or "Are those your rubber bands being stolen by a seagull?" The way you ask your questions will show your level of engagement in the conversation.

All these tips should help you improve your listening skills for comprehension. You can think of these as the foundation of becoming an active listener. That said, it is just as important to know what not to do during a conversation. More than anything else, you want to avoid habits associated with passive listening. There is a subtle difference between active and passive listening beyond engagement itself.

As you can likely surmise, passive listening is the polar opposite of active listening. It might as well be called *barely listening*. When you are a passive listener, you may be hearing what the other person is saying, but you are doing the bare minimum (perhaps nothing at all) to engage with the conversation, improve your comprehension, or adopt the perspective of the other person. In that sense, passive listening is about failing to extend the effort necessary to listen actively.

But more importantly, one habit closely associated with passive listening is the complete replacement of listening with the internal formulation of one's own response or argument. This is just another way to say that you are only waiting for your turn to speak. Instead of listening, you are preparing your response and disregarding the listening that you are supposed to be doing. When this happens, you fail to absorb almost anything that the other person has said, making constructive discourse nearly impossible. You may finally speak, but only to have the other person ask: *have you not been listening to anything I just said?*

Waiting for your turn to speak rather than listening is often a sign of your desire to "win"—or at least, dominate—the conversation. Though it is true that everyone wants to be heard and have their views received by others, internally working on your own argument while someone else is speaking shows a lack of interest in what they have to say as if you have nothing to learn from their point of view. If you do not care about what they are saying, then you probably do not actually want to engage in civil discourse. You simply want to argue and score points. But it must be said that this is not always a matter of intent. Many people are just accustomed to turning discourse into point-scoring argumentation. This is why ensuring you become an active listener is so vital. You have to want to actively listen, and you have to choose to do so. In choosing to be an active listener, you will see an immediate improvement in your interactions with others.

Active Listening Versus Passive Listening
QUESTIONS AND ANSWERS

Q: Is passive listening incompatible with civil discourse?

A: Passive listening doesn't do anything to improve discourse or enhance your understanding of new perspectives. In fact, it takes away from your ability to learn and grow. Therefore, if you consistently listen passively and refuse to change, then your behavior is largely incompatible with civil discourse.

But passive listening is something that most of us do from time to time. You may fall into passive listening habits for a few minutes, only to regain your focus and return your attention to discourse. Don't become frustrated with yourself and let that distract you; just try to get back on track with active listening. The most important thing to remember is that passive listening is not an insurmountable barrier to civil discourse, and you can always get back on track by returning to active listening.

One thing you can do if you zone out is apologize and tell the speaker you missed the last bit of what they said. Then, you give them a chance to repeat themselves, and you can make extra sure that you're intently focusing on what they say. You can be lighthearted and bond while laughing it off, or be soft and sincere if it's a more sensitive situation. Either way, most people will not be offended, but rather, they will appreciate your honesty. They'll be glad to have the chance to ensure that their message comes across.

Q: What should I do if I can't stop my mind from wandering during conversations?

A: Most of us struggle with wandering thoughts. It's a pretty natural thing that occurs in our minds—considering the average human has 6,200 thoughts per day.[13] Focusing on a discussion can be more difficult for some people, but pretty much everyone can overcome their irrelevant thought patterns when they occur. Mindfulness practice is a great way to increase your focus in general and work to prevent your mind from going to other places during discourse.

Q: Won't it seem strange if I repeat people's own words back to them?

A: Generally, repeating the last thing that someone said back to them is a sign that you are listening and want to understand them better. For most people, it will show your interest in their words. You don't need to directly repeat their exact words back to them—it's more like you're summarizing them. This process is sometimes called mirroring. If you think about people who are professional listeners, they engage in this behavior: impactful counselors reflect statements back to their patients, and excellent professors reword their students' questions before answering them for the class. Repeating a statement back to a speaker will actually begin to feel natural, and you will notice that the people around you respond well to that pattern of speech. Summarizing and sharing is a great way to build collaborative relationships. Let's look at an example.

You and a friend are discussing Amazon, the American multinational technology company famed for its algorithmically driven, next-day delivery system. They assert, "Well, I think it's just wrong. Amazon is a big corporation; they should do better to be good for people and the planet. They treat their workers terribly. They don't pay taxes. I think they're awful and irresponsible."

You might respond, "Okay, I hear what you're saying, and it's clear that corporate responsibility is important to you. Your frustrations with Amazon—that they don't treat their workers well or that you don't like how they handle taxes—make a lot of sense. I think corporate responsibility is important, too. But, I look at Amazon in a different way. . . ."

This example shows how you can repeat people's words back to them in a way that conveys that you've listened and makes them feel respected. But it also allows you to clarify ideas in a way to ensure clear communication so that you can keep the dialogue on track and productive. You are operating in good faith by representing their words back to them to show you understand.

BECOMING AN ACTIVE LISTENER

Like many aspects of civil discourse, active listening requires you to set aside your ego and try your hand at objective communication. You cannot read someone's thoughts, but you can read their body language, their tone, and the contents of their words. Whenever possible, you can ask questions to gain further clarification. But if you truly want to become an active listener, you have to set aside your personal motives or intentions when you listen.

In many ways, active listening is similar to the art of meditation. It may take time and practice. It will be worth it, though. It will let you cultivate the ability to clear your mind of judgments and personal motivations. You will be able to truly understand what someone else is trying to tell you. Once you have developed the ability to listen with the intention to understand from the perspective of another, you can practice active listening and greatly enhance your ability to engage in civil discourse. As an added bonus, becoming an active listener will be just one more mechanism in your communication toolkit.

While this may be disappointing for you to hear, there is no step-by-step guide to becoming an active listener. There are certain strategies you can implement to make the process easier (like clearing your mind, using the comprehension tips from the previous section, and continuously returning your focus to the speaker). However, this will not turn you into an active listener overnight. Everyone is different and will require their own unique approach. You just have to find out what best works for you and what suits your personality best.

More than anything else, you need to practice listening to others who are near you in the physical environment (not just "listen" to voice clips or text messages). More specifically, you need to practice listening in a setting that gives you the ability to respond. Listening to a podcast or watching the news puts you in an environment where you are not expected to respond as there is no one on the other end who can hear you. Therefore, your mind doesn't begin constructing a response because you know you won't need to interact. So to practice active listening, you need to take part in a live conversation with another person. This allows you to practice listening and, just as importantly, practice *not* speaking (and practice not formulating your next point as the other person is talking).

If you struggle with listening or you find it difficult to adopt the perspectives of other people, then you need to practice minimizing your speaking in the process. In doing so, most of what you say will come in the form of questions to extract new information, clear up gray areas, or simply show that you are actively engaged with what the other person is saying—demonstrating that you respect them and value them. During this sort of exercise, you should really think about listening (receptive) as the opposite of speaking (projective), as it is extremely difficult to do both at the same time.

Rather than getting bogged down in "winning" or articulating your point of view to sway someone else, listen to what others have to say. Oprah has spent her life listening and asking questions to dig just a little bit deeper. She doesn't try to defeat her opponents on the intellectual battlefield; she merely tries to understand them and, hopefully, gain a new perspective. Her style is a shining example of active listening being put into practice.

Becoming an Active Listener
QUESTIONS AND ANSWERS

Q: Doesn't active listening take away from my ability to contribute to civil discourse?

A: Without active listening, you cannot adequately contribute to civil discourse. If you fail to listen to other people and work to understand their positions, how could you hope to find truth or reach mutually beneficial results? While it is understandable to assume that you need to speak to make your point, it is important to remember that "making your point" is not the end goal of civil discourse. So try to listen first and formulate your personal opinions and counterpoints after you fully understand what has been said. Additionally, being an active listener doesn't mean *not* contributing; it just means not trying to do both at the same time. Of course, you have to engage in the conversation through speaking and hope that active listening is a two-way street. Balance and patience are key to successful civil discourse.

Q: How do I know when to speak and when not to speak?

A: There's no perfect script for having a productive back-and-forth with someone. Conversing is not a science, though science can play a part. It's more akin to an art, and it's something that forever unfolds and changes over the course of all your interactions. Sometimes, you should opt for silence and merely listen while other times you should voice your opinions and make yourself heard. If you're in a position where you do not know whether to speak or not, it is best to default to active listening and not speaking. Silence tends to give rise to the impulse to speak, but it's best not to speak if you think the other person is about to say something and is just being silent to find the right words. Even if the other person has finished their thought and there is a break in which you can provide your input, it is still often best to ask questions and encourage them to express themselves as completely as they can. This way, there is very little chance that you will misunderstand or misinterpret anything.

Q: What if the other person uses my silence to dominate the conversation?

A: In the event that someone speaks ad nauseam without allowing you to contribute, you always have the right to draw attention to the issue and work to express yourself adequately. Perhaps you are an introvert who is more selective about speaking. If so, try using a verbal signal to show that you want time to speak, such as "I'd like to have a moment to share my perspective here."

But even extroverts can be railroaded in conversations. In those cases, point out the other speaker's behavior in a calm but direct way. "I would appreciate it if I could make my point without interruption" or "Let's slow down so I can have a moment to make a point" are both options you could use.

But always remember: tone is essential. Don't let frustration cause you to take an aggressive or condescending tone. Smile. Relax your body, even when the other speaker escalates the energy level. If the other person refuses to allow you to contribute, then you always have the option to walk away from the conversation and try again another time.

DIFFERENT FORMS OF ACTIVE LISTENING

Thus far, I have looked at active listening in its most common form and by its most recognized definition: the auditory absorption of new information and perspectives. However, this would be a rather ableist point of view that discounts those with hearing disabilities. Moreover, the difficulty of reading body language for the visually impaired would make it seem as though true civil discourse is nearly impossible unless you possess unhindered senses and faculties.

Naturally, this is an absurd notion. One need only look to Helen Keller, one of the most accomplished deaf and blind women in human history. As a prolific writer, educator, and advocate for the disabled, Helen Keller took part in various debates and helped open up discourse to everyone. Examining a more recent example, Chella Man has had widespread influence as a deaf transgender actor, model, and LGBTQ activist. In his TED Talk, "Becoming Him,"[14] Chella Man discusses the difficulties associated with being deaf and transgender in a society that is not always accommodating to the former group, and frequently hostile to the latter. Through his YouTube channel, Chella Man has helped make it easier for the hearing impaired to overcome their difficulties and have open, sincere discourse without the need to "listen" in the traditional sense.

Helen Keller, Chella Man, and thousands of other outspoken people who deal with various disabilities show that listening is not just an auditory practice. It is using the faculties at your disposal to absorb information and work to understand the perspective of another person. This does not mean that you need to be able to see, hear, or speak. If you have the ability to take in new information, you have the ability to engage in discourse.

Technological advances have also empowered disabled people to "engage" even further in public discourse. Stephen Hawking, who suffered from ALS for most of his adult life, required advanced computers and devices to speak with others. Nonetheless, he was one of the most brilliant minds of the twentieth and twenty-first centuries. He had open debates and dialogues with others in academics, all while publishing some of the most respected works in the fields of physics and cosmology.

Physical disabilities are not the only reason that "listening" is a multifaceted concept. Some people simply absorb information better through reading or other formats. Long before the computer or even the telephone, some of the most profound discourses took place via "snail mail." Academics, politicians, philosophers, and theologians sent letters back and forth, sharing information and offering counterpoints with each subsequent dispatch. If nothing else, history has proven that written words require just as much "listening" as spoken ones.

Different Forms of Active Listening
QUESTIONS AND ANSWERS

Q: Can I really stop myself from forming knee-jerk judgments about things I hear or read?

A: In short, no. You cannot completely stop your brain from creating opinions or even judgments as soon as you read or hear something, especially if it's contrary to something you already believe. However, you can control how you respond to your own reaction. Just because you feel a sense of sadness, anger, frustration, or even indifference to tidbits of information does not mean that you need to succumb to those emotions and act them out wildly. Instead, you can take note of your reaction and ask yourself why you feel the way you feel. Then, you can work to take a more objective approach to the subject matter going forward.

Q: Having opinions is part of being human. Why should I suppress my opinions when I listen to others?

A: Active listening does not mean that you have to suppress your opinions. It simply means that you are delaying the expression of your thoughts until you have gathered sufficient information. Rather than reacting to an inflammatory statement with vitriol, wouldn't it be better to ask why it was said in the first place? If you can seek to understand the perspective of others, you can have much greater insights and offer opinions that go further than impulsive, often emotionally charged responses.

SUMMARY

Listening is an integral part of civil discourse. When you fail to listen, you fail to understand alternative perspectives. This inhibits your ability to engage in productive discourse and can often result in simply spouting your own views and ignoring the views of others. Through active listening, anyone can work toward understanding different intentions and perspectives. Additionally, prioritizing listening over speaking promotes a more civil and collaborative environment for everyone involved.

Remember these points to improve your active listening skills and enhance your ability to engage in discourse:

- Listen first, speak later—even if you want to lead a conversation, you should always make listening your first priority. This way, you ensure that everyone can share their views and you can enter the discussion as well-informed as possible.
- If you struggle to focus, use the practices outlined in this chapter to bring your mind back to the conversation at hand.
- Active listening is not just about hearing what someone is saying; it is about understanding the true intention and meaning behind their words—written or spoken. This will require you to temporarily set aside your own perspective and attempt to walk in the other person's shoes, even if only for a few moments.
- Remember that everyone wants to voice their opinion from time to time. Someone else's desire to speak is just as important as yours. Do not devalue what other people have to say, even if you disagree with them.

FINAL QUESTIONS AND ANSWERS

Q: Should I still practice active listening if someone is saying something harmful?

A: The degree to which a conversation is "harmful" will vary and will ultimately come down to your personal judgment. Just remember that there is a big difference between feeling off-put or offended and actually being in harm's way. Just having your feelings hurt is not harmful; sometimes harsh truths hurt. If a person is saying words that are difficult to hear for various reasons, you should still listen. Sometimes, people are mean-spirited and deliberately hurt others' feelings. However, it is up to you whether to let that control your emotions, and you can take the steps necessary to deal with the matter that presents itself. Sure, you can feel hurt by what someone says, and you are within your rights to stand up against it in the most respectful manner that the situation calls for.

Know that harmful discourse is unacceptable: racist, sexist, homophobic, transphobic, anti-Semitic, Islamophobic, or anti-immigrant speech does not have a place in civil discourse. Speech born from hate cannot ever be civil. If a conversation becomes harmful or dangerous, there is a point where active listening becomes moot. If the conversation becomes hostile, hateful, or threatens someone's safety, you should naturally abandon active listening and focus on creating a safe, civil environment for yourself and others.

Chapter Six
Being Attentive

Listening and being attentive are like two branches of the same tree. As I touched on in the last chapter, part of listening is showing the speaker that you are, in fact, listening. You can do this with your words, facial expressions, and posture. This means that, much like listening, being attentive is something that you can (and should) do whether you are communicating face-to-face or in written format. It's also a skill you can hone and practice. Regardless of the communication format, attentiveness is both a necessary part of keeping discourse civil and a way to enhance the productivity of the discussion at hand.

THE ATTENTIVE PARTICIPANT

"What do you mean it's better?" I said.

Terrence looked over at me, slightly taken aback. "Well, first of all . . ."

"Nope," I said, shaking my head. "The second *Jurassic Park* is way better than the first. *The Lost World* is so good!"

A small smile appeared on Terrence's face. "I'm not saying it's bad. I'm just saying the first has a magic that couldn't be replicated."

"What's more magical than a T-Rex stomping through San Diego?"

"How about when Dr. Alan Grant first sees a living dinosaur?"

"Nope, Jeff Goldblum is the real star of the franchise. Everyone knows that."

"He's in the first *Jurassic Park*, too, though."

I shook my head. "How could you think *Jurassic Park* is better than *The Lost World?* That's a ridiculous belief."

Like many young adults, I spent my years in college assuming that I knew more than many of those around me. Some of this was arrogance, but some of it was also a way of protecting myself from complex discussions that challenged my mind's status quo. In these situations, I could not be an active listener, but just as importantly, I was projecting my lack of attentiveness onto the conversation and creating even further misunderstanding. This led to many, many unproductive conversations that could have easily turned uncivil under slightly different circumstances. Fortunately, with time spent focusing on civil discourse, I began to see how destructive I was being in many of my conversations. I started working toward becoming an attentive participant in discourse. I still struggle with attentiveness from time to time, but the more importance I give to being an active and attentive participant, the more I can do to promote civil discourse in my daily life.

I do wonder the reasons why I was so high on myself. I took a combative and competitive approach to conversation, and I thought that it was important for me to be right—and for other people to *know* that I was right. I'm not sure who I was trying to impress, but I took it personally if someone had an alternative viewpoint. I was one of those people who would think, *How could you possibly think that?* without ever stopping to truly listen, ask, or understand why people may come to different conclusions. I wasn't attentive to other people's points at all because I thought it was more important that they be attentive to mine.

Andrew Wilkinson, the co-founder of the venture capital firm Tiny, took to Twitter in early 2022 to share his thoughts on being attentive and engaged in conversation. He had this to say:

> Most people are garbage during conversation. People don't realize that it's not what you SAY that makes others like you. It's about how you make the other person FEEL when they're with you. What you give THEM space to say . . . The question you asked that nobody else has ever asked them. The interest you showed in what they shared. What they feel in their gut when you smile and nod. That you genuinely care and like and understand them. That they feel seen. Most people view conversations as one way. They focus on sounding smart and saying interesting things. What they should be focused on is asking interesting and unique questions. Figuring out what someone is passionate about and getting them talking about it . . . I'd say at least half of the conversations I have are one-way. People grab the mic and deliver a monologue. They focus on saying smart things. They talk 80% of the time. And I've noticed that some of the world's most successful people naturally do the opposite. They don't over-talk. They ask questions.

They show interest. They make the other person feel special. Try it next time. Focus on asking questions of the other person, you'll be surprised what happens.[15]

These tips and observations may seem obvious to some, but most people are completely unaware of how they attempt to project their own interests and values, figuratively (and sometimes, literally) shouting down others just to have their point heard. The lack of attentiveness is one of the catalysts to the current state of division in the United States and the world at large. When people do not feel heard, they do not feel valued. They feel as though they have to scream just to be noticed. At the societal level, this can lead to resentment toward those who are "not listening" or refusing to consider ideas. Over time, a lack of attentiveness across the political spectrum only increases divisiveness and extremism, especially when people decide more and more that the other will never listen. The people who don't feel they are listened to, in turn, decide to not listen to others. It's an unfortunate and self-propagating cycle when everyone refuses to listen.

But Andrew Wilkinson and others have caught onto the idea that people don't just want to be heard; they want to feel a positive response when they are speaking. Or, at the very least, they want to feel as though their opinions, thoughts, feelings, and words are not met with immediate hostility or thoughtless retorts. This is where attentiveness diverges from active listening. While active listening requires a degree of attentive behavior, it is not a requirement. One can sit quietly, listen, and absorb information without taking steps to make the other person feel safe and comfortable. Attentiveness requires you to go one step further.

Imagine you and your friend, Marcia, are sitting down for coffee at the local coffee shop. "So, what's up?" you ask.

Marcia sighs. "I'm okay, I guess." She stares into her coffee mug. You nod. "That's good."

"It's just that guy I've been seeing, Clarence."

"Uh-huh." You glance up, examining an abstract piece of artwork on the wall. It looks like some sort of animal—like a bat meets a giraffe.

"I do like him, but I don't see a future with him. We're just so different."

"Right," you say. You look away from the odd artwork and briefly look at her. She's rubbing the side of her face with her hand. You turn and look around the coffee shop.

"I don't want to hurt him, but I feel like breaking up would be the best thing for both of us."

You instinctively reach for your phone and open your email to check if your coworker responded to your question from the day before. "Yeah, that makes sense."

"It will be hard at first, but I think it's for the best. What do you think?"

You look up from your phone and shrug. "Gotta do what you gotta do." You sip your drink and grimace , saying, "Does your coffee taste . . . weirdly burnt to you?"

This doesn't seem very attentive, does it? So what *does* an attentive participant look like in practice?

Imagine you and your friend Marcia are sitting down for coffee at the local coffee shop. "So, what's up?" you ask.

Marcia sighs. "I'm okay, I guess." She stares into her coffee mug. You pause. "Okay? That's . . . good?"

"It's just that guy I've been seeing, Clarence."

"Okay, tell me more . . ." You glance up, examining an abstract piece of artwork on the wall. It looks like some sort of animal—like a bat meets a giraffe. You catch your breath and refocus.

"I do like him, but I don't see a future with him. We're just so different."

"What kinds of differences are you noticing?" you ask, repeating her words back to her so that she can feel that you're listening.

In its simplest form, attentive behavior requires care and compassion for what someone else is saying. It requires you to make others feel comfortable while speaking, which goes beyond just listening; it is about the behavior you project onto the conversation as someone else is speaking. This can be accomplished through positive body language and, perhaps most importantly, interest and enthusiasm in the other participant(s).

The Attentive Participant
QUESTIONS AND ANSWERS

Q: How do I know if I'm being attentive?

A: Humans often exchange subtle messages without the need for detailed explanations. You can tell that you are being an attentive participant when the other person shows signs of comfort and ease when speaking. Alternatively, if they seem closed off to conversation, hesitant to share information, or to engage in discourse, you should work harder to make them feel safe to speak and converse with you. Listening and showing interest are two effective methods, but asking questions that show your interest in the other person can also help close gaps between participants. Having an open and friendly body posture is another way to create comfort and show attentiveness.

For example, if you are in a conversation and you realize you're monologuing, or you've lost someone because you're speaking deeply about a topic you love and they don't fully understand, and you notice them shift in their seat, there are a couple of things you can do. You can either ask them a direct question about some of the stuff you're talking about, and how they feel about the topic, or you can switch it up and ask, "So how are things with you anyway? What have you been doing in the last week?" and then ask further probing questions from there.

Q: How exactly is being an attentive participant different from being an active listener?

A: Though the two practices go hand in hand, they ultimately achieve different goals through slightly different methods. Active listening means focusing on new information and giving others the space to speak. Being attentive means making the other person feel comfortable and safe to express themselves without fear of judgment or ridicule. Being an attentive participant is a bonus and positive upgrade from just being an active listener. It means that you are actively ensuring the other person understands that they can speak their mind freely and feels comfortable in doing so.

ATTENTIVENESS, CONTACT THEORY, AND CIVIL DISCOURSE

In 2003, David Isay founded StoryCorps. At the time, it was a small project headquartered in New York City's Grand Central Terminal. Isay would give random people the opportunity to record their stories with the goal of creating a library of American oral history. Today, David Isay has recorded the stories and experiences of more than half a million people, making StoryCorps the largest single collection of human voices ever recorded.

While documenting oral histories offers unique and invaluable insights into different cultures and epochs, StoryCorps had even higher aspirations since its earliest days. Isay believes that now more than ever, people feel misunderstood and judged. By collecting stories and making them available to people through NPR and even as animated shorts, he has helped share stories that would go untold in more traditional media outlets. Moreover, he gives people the chance to tell their own stories with their own voices, unaltered or manipulated by others and unframed by the constraints of a sixty-second or five-minute news segment.

In recent years, public discourse has only deteriorated further, particularly within the realm of American politics. This spurred

David Isay to create an offshoot project under StoryCorps called "One Small Step." Rather than simply allowing one person to share their personal stories, One Small Step puts two people on opposite ends of the political spectrum together to speak for fifty minutes. Each session begins with one person reading a brief biography of the other person. Then, they are able to talk about whatever they like. With each new recording, Isay has found that even people who seemingly have nothing in common have been able to overcome their political differences and have civil discussions. In an interview with *60 Minutes*, Isay explained part of the reason why he thinks that One Small Step has been so successful:

> I think people feel misunderstood and judged. You know, in the history of humanity, nobody's ever changed their mind by being called an idiot or a moron or a snowflake. But, you know, many minds have been changed by being listened to, by conversation, being told that they're loved.[16]

This is simply attentiveness in practice: people showing compassion and care for others, in spite of their differences, to make them feel comfortable, safe, heard, and even loved. And though he may be at the forefront of trying to change people's perspectives one person (or two people) at a time, David Isay is not the first person to stumble upon the benefits of attentiveness. In fact, contact theory has been a focus of various independent and state-funded studies since the 1950s. While there are various complex psychological factors at play, researchers have found that controlled interactions between groups of people with different political backgrounds, religions, or ethnicities can help reduce prejudices between majority and minority groups.

This shows that direct contact and interaction with people who have different views or backgrounds can help reduce negative feelings toward them. Perhaps it's because people make so many assumptions about those who they perceive as different from them. We have a natural propensity to adhere to "ingroups"' and "outgroups." When people are in the same room discussing an issue with one another while using active listening and being attentive, real breakthroughs can occur. Naturally, this isn't always the case. Sometimes, prejudice and hatred run very deep and cannot be undone by a glorified group therapy session. Unlearning patterns can take months or years—or never happen at all. However, when the effects of contact theory are combined with active listening and attentiveness, it can greatly increase the chances of civil discourse taking place, regardless of how the participants felt about one another beforehand. And, well, we've got to start somewhere.

APPLYING CONTACT THEORY IN BUSINESS: STARTING *THE DOE*

I started *The Doe* after college, having grown fed up with the lack of discourse on campus. I had writing experience with *The Huffington Post* and had written about the agricultural industry since high school. I had also written a 2017 article about how we could bridge the gap between Democrats and Republicans by first realizing that we all had common ground. In the article, I said, "It would be easy to assume that we have nothing in common, but that's just not true. Both of us consider ourselves patriots, both of us support helping nations in need, and both of us feel that more should be done to help the less fortunate in the United States."[17] All of these writing experiences shaped a need to address issues writers struggle with.

I founded *The Doe* because I felt held back. I was apprehensive about posting anything because I feared the inevitable backlash. So I created a publication that allowed writers to share their opinions without fear of online attacks.

We launched during the George Floyd protests of 2020—a tumultuous time for our country. People were taking to the streets because they didn't feel heard, so I decided that it would be best to publish marginalized perspectives—usually things that were counter to the dominant narrative. So, one person we published was a Black conservative who did not agree with the Black Lives Matter (BLM) protests. He wrote that he didn't feel that the statistics backed up what was being said about systemic racism.

We didn't publish him just to publish the counternarrative, though. We published another piece alongside it, one from someone on the frontlines of the BLM protests, and someone who deeply supported the cause. We wanted to juxtapose multiple viewpoints to encourage all readers to think about the complexity of these powerful moments in history.

These stories got our publication a lot of attention, which was great, though a lot of that attention was from people who were angry. We saw some excellent discourse in the comment section about—crucially—why there was so much anger. Ultimately, that was okay. My point in publishing these stories was to show that these perspectives existed. Not publishing the stories would not have meant those viewpoints didn't exist; we didn't create the experiences, we just gave a forum for sharing them.

When running a publishing company, I knew not everyone would agree with everything I did. But arguing without listening, especially from behind a screen, doesn't solve any issue. While bullying has certainly been around since the first Neanderthal made fun of his neighbor for not making fire, social media has made aggression toward other people much easier. When you're writing from behind a screen, it can give you the boldness to say what you want to say. That's not a bad thing! Of course, that's why I started *The Doe* in the first place. But the stories we published weren't about targeting individuals with incivility or with an intent to tear people down.

That's why contact theory is so important. Looking into someone's eyes while seeing that they are a human being with an emotional response to the words you say is one way to ensure that your discourse is civil. Talking in person is not always possible when discussing online or writing an article, but you can still be aware of the human element when you communicate in these situations.

Applying Contact Theory in Business
QUESTIONS AND ANSWERS

Q: What are some ways that I can apply contact theory to my own life?

A: Again, there's a reason so much meaningful discourse has been had over shared meals: from the Last Supper to the salons of the Enlightenment. Even remote working teams can meet for annual conferences or break bread together in a Zoom room to have an opportunity to be in direct contact and build discursive bonds. Coaches can ensure sports teams get together in the off-season to maintain the listening and collaborative skills needed to win as a team. Even reviving your extended family dinner, book clubs, or "college friends' brunch" traditions that were put on hold during the pandemic are opportunities to practice contact theory and attentiveness and to create moments of civil discourse.

MAKING OTHERS FEEL COMFORTABLE

It is easy to just say that attentiveness is a good quality that encourages true civil discourse, but what does it look like in a real-life conversation? What are attentive behaviors and practices? More than anything else, attentiveness is linked with kindness and compassion. In other words, if you can be polite, courteous, kind, and compassionate to someone else—even if you disagree with them— you have taken the most important step toward being an attentive participant in civil discourse.

However, attentiveness is not all about pleasantries. One of the keys to being attentive is making the other person feel *comfortable*. Most people feel comfortable when they can talk about something that they enjoy. Asking questions about someone's personal hobbies, interests, passions, or areas of expertise can help open up dialogue, particularly when the other person appears apprehensive to speak. Attentiveness means starting a conversation off with a connection, and you should take it upon yourself to find a way to connect to the person you're talking to. If you don't know anything about this person, just try something along the lines of "So what are you into?" or

"Is every piece of furniture in your house made of toothpicks, or just these pieces here in the living room?" Yep, sometimes, it's as simple as that. You can then riff off their answer (or ask another question if they find it difficult to answer) to probe even deeper.

Once you have found one or more topics that help the other person feel more comfortable, it's your chance to be an active listener. Truly listen and show interest in what is being said through your body language. You don't even have to speak. Simply leaning forward, nodding, making eye contact, and uncrossing your arms can let the other person know that you care about what they say.

Naturally, when the opportunity arises, you can chime in with relevant anecdotes or experiences that you share with the other person. However, listening is always more important than talking. And showing interest and openness to what you're hearing will greatly increase the chances of making the other person feel safe and comfortable to speak their mind.

Why does it matter so much to make people feel comfortable and safe? Because, according to David Isay, we are currently living in a "culture of contempt." People often enter dialogues assuming the absolute worst of the other person. They do not expect to be heard or respected. Instead, they anticipate vitriol and hatred if they express themselves freely. So people either choose not to say anything that might cause conflict, or they enter the discussion with an aggressive, dominant stance—with the hope that this will help shield them against "attacks" from "the other side."

Also, you can feel vulnerable entering a conversation with anyone, whether they're a stranger or not. We want to connect to others, but we feel that not attempting to connect is better than trying to connect and having our efforts shot down. If we operate from a place of fear, then we might end up silencing ourselves or fail to listen to others who say something we disagree with. Operating in fear means we aren't feeling comfortable or we aren't making others feel comfortable.

In times like these, making people feel safe and secure can actually come as quite a shock to them. It can completely change the trajectory of your discourse. Even a small joke to lighten the mood can help put someone else at ease, demonstrating that you're going to be collaborative with them in the conversation. Show you're not a threat—even if you have different opinions.

One problem you might encounter with your kindness, however, is that the other person may think that you're trying to trap them by "pretending" to be kind and attentive. However, if you are persistent, you can show that you truly want to engage in a civil, respectful dialogue. This opens people up to share their true feelings—hopefully without the desire to hurt or offend you in turn. Even if they continue to act aggressively, it will become harder and harder for them to maintain an aggressive stance when you are showing kindness and a consistent willingness to listen and learn.

Making Others Feel Comfortable
QUESTIONS AND ANSWERS

Q: What if I feel uncomfortable during a conversation?

A: Civil discourse can make people uncomfortable. You may have to confront ideas or even personal experiences that can be difficult. That said, you should not let other people disrespect you or make you feel like you don't have value in the conversation. So do your best to distinguish between discomfort caused by topics and discomfort caused by mistreatment. Either way, you should not abandon your attentiveness to get *revenge*. This will only escalate uncivil conversations.

And remember, if you need to step away from a conversation that doesn't feel safe, you should not feel afraid to do so. Exiting uncivil discourse is better than perpetuating it. You can say something like "I'm sorry, but I'd prefer to end this conversation. Have a great day," in a tone that's friendly but firm and leads you out of the conversation. If it's with someone you know better, or a family member you live with, for example, you can go for something along the lines of "This conversation is really frustrating me, and I would like to stop talking for now. Love you." Again, firm but fair.

Q: Isn't talking about other people's favorite topics a waste of time?

A: When you think of civil discourse, you often think of important topics debated in a respectful way. However, you cannot always get straight to the "respectful" part without putting in the work first. This means getting to know the other person and making a human connection with them. By talking about topics that interest them and showing enthusiasm in the conversation, you can make it far easier to discuss other topics freely and productively. Taking the time for attentiveness will pay off in the long run.

SUMMARY

Attentiveness shows your commitment to engaging in civil discourse in a genuine and respectful manner. If you do not take the time to show respect and interest in your discursive counterpart, you may find the conversation hitting a wall quickly. However, by listening, showing interest, and being kind and respectful, you can form a human connection—helping both parties overcome prejudices. Just as importantly, attentiveness can help make everyone feel safe and comfortable to speak their minds without fear of judgment.

Remember these points to improve your attentiveness during discourse:

- Focus on making the other person *feel* heard. This requires you to do more than just listen. You will need to show enthusiasm for the conversation and give the other person ample time to express themselves adequately.

- Understand that most people feel unheard or misunderstood. Actively working to understand others will encourage them to treat you fairly in kind.
- Take note of your word choice and body language. You shouldn't be afraid to confront uncomfortable topics, but you should work to make others feel safe to speak.
- Try to help others open up and feel comfortable by asking questions. This can help turn slow or unproductive conversations into more effective discourse.

FINAL QUESTIONS AND ANSWERS

Q: What should I do if I'm not truly interested or enthused about what someone has to say?

A: Civil discourse often involves the exchange of opposing ideas. This means that you may not always like what you hear. However, if you truly wish to learn and grow through discourse, you may have to "fake it till you make it" when it comes to enthusiasm. Showing interest and enthusiasm during a conversation is a lot like smiling to make yourself happy. Even if you don't feel happy at first, the simple act of smiling can actually make you feel better. Similarly, showing interest and enthusiasm in a conversation can actually make you engage with the conversation more, your enthusiasm to become more real and genuine. Even if you disagree with someone's points, you are still eager to hear them and understand them so that you can advance the conversation. So bring that energy and eagerness to create more attentiveness.

Q: Doesn't attentiveness encourage self-censorship and discourage honest dialogue?

A: Being attentive doesn't mean that you have to stop yourself from being honest or saying how you really feel. However, you can't expect to jump straight into a conversation without developing a comfortable, safe rapport with another person. This is especially true when two people have vast differences of opinion. There may be a tendency to enter the conversation in an aggressive or hostile way. Being attentive can help keep discourse civil and respectful while still giving you the power to speak honestly and openly.

Chapter Seven
Maintaining Focus

My body flailed as the horse I rode galloped away from the others. I could hear the calls from my father and sister getting farther and farther away behind me. My heart thumped in my throat. The trees in the distance blurred into a greenish brown. I twisted my body, trying to regain control, but we were going too fast. The saddle slid sideways and so did I.

Freefall.

Crack.

The world around me went dark. When I opened my eyes, my dad was crouching over me, out of breath.

"Are you okay?"

I was fine. In fact, I wanted to do it again.

Though I still have a 6.7 mm protruding disc in my back due to the incident, the thrill of understanding the unknown only made me more excited to ride horses.

Horses are a lot like humans in many ways. They can get distracted. They may lash out if they feel threatened. You can communicate with them, even if that communication, of course, looks different from how you would communicate with your neighbor, grandma, or mailman (I would assume, at least). Horses sometimes respond to vocal cues, like "whoa," but there are physical cues that are often more important. The way you move your legs can help spur your beastly companion forward, and pulling on the reins tells your horse to slow down. The two of you have to be in tune with each other.

A key communication tool when riding horses is patting the horse when you can feel it starting to get anxious. If you're not aware of your horse, you may not think to scratch its back to show that it's safe. Being unaware of your horse might mean you accidentally kicked it too hard in its side, sending it tearing across the field.

You, and your horse, need focus to succeed.

The modern world often draws our attention in a million different directions, just like how the many stimuli tug at a horse's attention. It's like different threads appearing all around us, and each tries to pull a different part of our minds to pay attention to something else. Advertisers know this. The makers of your smart televisions, phones, social media sites, and all else know it. Even maintaining a single conversation can be difficult when you feel your phone buzzing in your pocket, you hear your favorite song playing somewhere nearby, conversations are happening all around you, or you just allow your mind to wander and get lost in one of your many daily worries. But you can't actively listen or be attentive if you are distracted by your surroundings. For this reason, working on maintaining focus is paramount during civil discourse. While there are plenty of modern methods of improving focus, some of the best methods can be drawn from ancient traditions and practices.

Let us return to Japan and learn about some more Eastern philosophy.

THE JAPANESE TRADITION OF *ICHIGYO ZAMMAI*

If you're not familiar with *Ichigyo Zammai,* you are not alone. In the Western world, it is still a rather obscure ancient Japanese practice that is closely associated with Zen Buddhism. Despite existing in some parts of the world for thousands of years, Ichigyo Zammai is still one of the best-kept Japanese secrets and an effective way to improve your ability to focus.

Rather than being a complex activity, Ichigyo Zammai deals in simplicity. It refers to the practice of focusing on one single act at a time by clasping one of the world's "threads" for extended periods. While it sounds easy enough to do, most people struggle with focusing on just one thing at a time (especially in our modern age). I've—no joke—caught myself with the television on, listening to music in headphones, looking at a video on my laptop, and scrolling through social media on my phone. Am I the only one who's felt like a power strip with a few too many devices plugged into it—about to blow a fuse? How can a human mind cope with this amount of stimuli? It can't.

Ichigyo Zammai is naturally intertwined with the concept of being completely "present" in the current moment. When you are eating, you are just focused on the act of eating—no televisions blaring in the background, no texting—just the flavors, smells, textures, sights, sounds, and tactile experience of your meal. When you are speaking, you are just focused on the act of speaking. And even when you are walking, you are just focused on the act of walking—one leg in front of the other. There's nothing else for you to do but the single task at hand.

Of course, this may feel a little extreme to people who like to multitask—which is actually "task switching." Instead of working on multiple things at once, task switchers jump between tasks very quickly. It's not the optimal way to function but is somewhat of a demand from our modern world.

Personally, I like to take in lots of different kinds of information in quick succession. One minute, I might be writing an article as I wait to start a video call with my sister. In between both, I'll likely scroll through my newsfeed to stay up-to-date on the latest trends. During most of these little moments that happen throughout the day, my mind is constantly on the move. Thoughts jump from one thing to the next. Through dozens of conversations with friends, family, and colleagues, I've learned that I'm not alone. The human brain moves a lot faster than we do physically, and when you add in the constant external stimuli of the modern world (emails, social media, etc.), it can be difficult to just focus on one thing at a time. But focus we must because inside true focus can come a state of consciousness that makes us feel more connected, clearheaded, and involved than ever.

This is why the practice of Ichigyo Zammai requires a conscious decision to focus and can be a slowed-down antidote to the poison of our sped-up world. It also requires a lot of practice. You can't just say, "I'm going to be focused from now on" and expect it to have any real effect. Instead, you need to cultivate the ability to focus on one thing at a time. Before trying to apply this practice to civil discourse, it's best to start with small tasks to make this lifelong task more bite-sized and more manageable.

Perhaps you're cutting vegetables in preparation for dinner.

Peel the carrots.

Sharpen the knife.

Get out the cutting board.

How much celery do I need?

Wait, where'd I put the carrots?

Oh, they're on the counter. Speaking of which, I should clean the counter. I need to vacuum, too, and might as well clean the shower.

Wait, I was preparing something . . . was it that email to Cynthia? Did I file that report she asked me to take care of?

Rather than thinking about what you need to do around the house or what you forgot to do at work the other day, simply focus on the task you are doing. If you are cutting a carrot, only focus on the act of cutting the carrot. Feel the weight of the knife in your one hand and the wetness of the carrot in the other. Listen to the carrot split as you press the blade into it. Watch how you turn it into little orange pieces of nutritious goodness. If external thoughts or distractions attempt to work their way in, do your best to continue focusing on the task at hand, however unimportant it may seem.

Carrot.

Knife.

Cutting board.

Carrot.

Knife.

Cutting board.

Better, right?

After years of assuming that multitasking was the best way to amp up my productivity and get the most out of everything I did, I came across Ichigyo Zammai. I won't go as far as saying that it changed my life forever, but I will say that it has made me more conscious of where my attention lies at any given moment. It has also helped me realize that just because modern life is fast-paced does not mean that I need to approach every task with lightning speed and with my thoughts already moving before I've even started. I've learned that I don't need to think about the next task or the task after that before I've finished what's in front of me.

Instead, I find myself much more calm when I'm able to achieve singular focus. I can dedicate more attention to detail when I push myself to concentrate on one act at a time. It's also important to note what that "task" or "act" can feel like in rather broad terms. In this context, they should refer to very specific actions. So if you are working on a project for work, that may involve dozens or even hundreds of different actions. Break down what you are doing into its most basic forms, and tackle each with focus. Not only will this help you stay present as you take each and every step toward your goal of finishing the project, but it will also help you achieve your overarching objectives without being paralyzed by a task that's too large.

Let me use writing *I'm Just Saying* as an example. Of course, my goal was to write the book, but if I always thought about needing a full book over and over, it would have made my task far more difficult. If someone were to ask me, "I've never written a book before; where do you suggest I start?" I'd say, "Start with a simple story." Most of us have the ability to write a first sentence. Once we do that, we can focus on the next one—perhaps even thinking about a whole paragraph until we work through sections and chapters. When we chunk tasks like this, it is far easier to discipline ourselves into either writing a certain number of words in a sitting (let's say 500) each day, or to put on a thirty-minute or one-hour timer for uninterrupted writing time.

Finally, focusing is like a muscle. We can train it. If we focus on tasks we want to do or love doing, we can train ourselves to listen more intently when we are conversing. Therefore, focus is at the cornerstone of civil discourse. Rather than going too much more into detail about this topic, let's look into Ichigyo Zammai more deeply.

Ichigyo Zammai
QUESTIONS AND ANSWERS

Q: Does Ichigyo Zammai require any special training to master?

A: Thankfully, the answer is no! You can start practicing Ichigyo Zammai without any special training or knowledge. All it takes is persistence, determination, and practice on a daily basis. That said, if you want to learn more about the ancient tradition and the philosophy behind it, you can learn more in Sunryu Suzuki's book *Zen Mind, Beginner's Mind*.

Q: Won't focusing on one task at a time make me oblivious to what's going on around me?

A: In some cases, focusing on the task at hand can make you so laser focused that you lose track of things happening on the periphery. Some call this the "flow" state, or being in the zone. When you are in this state you can lose all track of time and be quite lost in the enjoyment of your task as your conscious mind fades into the background and a deeper part of yourself takes over.

However, this doesn't mean that you will be oblivious to external factors. With enough practice, you can cultivate the ability to distinguish between important and unimportant external stimuli without losing focus on what you are doing. If you do find yourself distracted by external stimuli rather than losing focus entirely, you can learn to redirect your focus to the task at hand. Instead of getting frustrated, for example, take a deep breath through your nose, exhale, and go back to what you are doing. Life is full of distractions, noises, and interruptions.

Like that weird spot on the wall that looks like Jamie Lee Curtis!

Where was I? Oh, right! To take a more Zen-like approach would be to accept that there are things happening around you and to move forward regardless. That being said, it's a powerful practice to eliminate as many distractions as possible, too.

Q: Okay, this sounds good, but when my phone . . .

A: I'm going to stop you right there. Studies have shown that cell phones, especially when used for mindless scrolling, break our concentration and focus.[18] Some people try app blockers to temporarily block all but the most essential notifications on their phones. I've found that putting my "doom-scrolling" apps in a folder at the top of my screen—far from easy finger access—helps me use the apps for much less time and more intentionally. Do-not-disturb functions are great, too.

But the relentless dings from our phones—from someone tapping a heart beneath a photo of our cars on social media—are antithetical to calming the mind. Focusing on just one activity at a time most likely means releasing yourself from the phone altogether, even if for a short period of time.

Let's go back to the book example. If I create a small aim to write 500 words of this book at a time, the best thing to do is turn off my phone and put it in a drawer. Because I'm a CEO or chairman of multiple companies, this is sometimes not possible. There may be something urgent that happens in one of my businesses that demands my focus. However, the elimination of phone distractions, not having multiple tabs open on my browser, and generally sitting myself in a quiet place goes a long way in helping me feel less distracted.

Social media and our technology in general has trained us to do the opposite of quieting and stilling the mind: our world is always scrolling, switching between feeds, and liking and commenting on one thing after the next. Things fill, but nothing fulfills. Ichigyo Zammai is an opportunity to free yourself from that training and reclaim control over how you approach focus.

Q: What about focusing on a conversation?

A: When you give someone your focus, using the active listening principles from Chapter 5 and being attentive from Chapter 6, you are likely to be in a calmer, more receptive state to someone else's ideas. You will be more receptive to their humaneness, too.

In *Zen Mind, Beginner's Mind,* Sunryu Suzuki states,

> When you listen to someone, you should give up all your preconceived ideas and your subjective opinions; you should just listen to him, just observe what his way is. We put very little emphasis on right and wrong or good and bad. We just see things as they are with him, and accept them. This is how we communicate with each other. Usually when you listen to some statement, you hear it as a kind of echo of yourself. You are actually listening to your

own opinion. If it agrees with your opinion you may accept it, but if it does not, you will reject it or you may not even really hear it.[19]

Heed this view as you go into conversations, as it will help deepen constructive dialogue.

MINDFULNESS MEDITATION

Implementing Ichigyo Zammai in your life can be difficult, especially if you are accustomed to thinking about a dozen different goals or issues every few seconds. If you're anything like me, your natural inclination is like that of a hummingbird confronted with a hundred flowers, darting swiftly between each one. While practicing Ichigyo Zammai in your daily life is the best way to improve your focus, it is not the only way for you to enhance it. As a proponent of mindfulness meditation, I have worked to relax my mind and focus on the present moment. Too often, our minds can give us rushing, anxious thoughts about the future, or depressing, regretful thoughts about the past. Focusing on the present, and seeing it as being all there is in that moment, can bring a sense of calm to that hummingbird mind.

Much like Ichigyo Zammai, meditation dates back centuries and has its roots in religious practices—notably Buddhism and Hinduism. Practicing mindfulness meditation also can make Ichigyo Zammai easier and, in turn, help you become more focused and present during all activities—including civil discourse. Why? Because it cultivates the calmness and carefulness that's essential to this type of discourse through teaching you how to stay calm, no matter what issue or challenge you're faced with.

We talked about how meditation can assist in self-reflection, but it's relevant when it comes to focus, too. There are various approaches to meditation, but I think it is important to first take note of the word *mindfulness*. This term is frequently tossed around in irrelevant contexts, which has started to make it lose its meaning. Nonetheless, I think that mindfulness is an extremely important concept and discipline that, when used properly, can help people identify internal hurdles, overcome difficult emotional states, and attain a greater sense of spiritual oneness with the world. When it comes to focusing and engaging in civil discourse, mindfulness meditation is one of the best ways to actively practice being present and push away unrelated or unproductive thoughts.

Like Ichigyo Zammai, mindfulness meditation is not something that requires a guru, religious conviction, or even any external help. You simply practice focusing your mind on your breathing—bringing you to a place of quiet, peaceful contemplation. In that way, mindfulness can be both secular, spiritual, religious, or a combination of the three. You can take the psychological angle or the spiritual angle; the bottom line is that, for most of us, mindfulness meditation works to improve how we feel about life and how we conduct ourselves in the world at large.

Also, like Ichigyo Zammai, mindfulness meditation takes a lot of practice, and you won't always end a meditation session feeling "successful." That's okay, though. It's solitary—not a game of solitaire. Every time you sit down, you are having success in the sense that you're doing something that moves you toward mindfulness. Although sometimes the meditative state is easy to get into and you get where you want to be instantly, other times it's more elusive than that. You may not experience that ease of relaxation. But that's okay; you can't control every aspect of every day. Therefore, you can't control every aspect of meditation, either. My advice is that you set an intention, like "I will experience calmness" or "I will feel compassion toward my father," before you start meditating. This can prime you to get into that liberating state of mind more easily, but again, it's never a guarantee.

I remember the first few times that I tried to meditate, I was overcome with a flood of thoughts and feelings that I couldn't push away. For a while, I abandoned meditation entirely. I assumed I wasn't cut out for it. I thought it was just for people who were naturally good at it, and I didn't see it as a skill anyone could cultivate.

Fortunately, I came back to it after speaking with other entrepreneurs who had nothing but positive things to say about it. And it wasn't just what they were saying that changed my mind, but the entirety of their being—their body language, calmness in speaking, and general demeanor was different—in a good way. They seemed more alive, more vibrant, more present, and more open to listening. Though there could have been a variety of factors at play, they all attributed these changes to meditation. So, I gave it another shot.

After weeks and weeks of meditating on a daily basis, I started to experience a difference. I felt more at peace with myself and more able to focus on the present moment. It helped me engage in conversations without digressing or getting distracted by outside forces. As weeks turned into months and months into years, I saw that mindfulness meditation helped make me a better communicator. I am more in tune with myself, which has enabled me to become more empathic and open to others.

Mindfulness Meditation
QUESTIONS AND ANSWERS

Q: Do I have to meditate to maintain focus during civil discourse?

A: Absolutely not. Mindfulness meditation is a tactic to improve your sense of self and enhance your focus on the present moment. It gives you a sense of control to quiet your mind and helps you engage in active listening. However, you can still be a completely active participant in civil discourse without ever even attempting to meditate. But if you struggle to focus on daily tasks or you find your mind wandering during conversations, mindfulness meditation could help center your focus going forward.

Q: How does mindfulness meditation improve focus?

A: Meditation pushes you to focus your mind by paying attention to your breathing rather than anything else that pops into your mind. Mindfulness meditation specifically helps you slow down or even stop intrusive thoughts so you can focus better on the present moment. In doing so, you can learn useful practices for focusing your mind even when you are not actively engaged in meditation. This will allow you to be a more active listener and be more attentive to those you speak with. This is what makes meditation so useful for those who want to improve their engagement in civil discourse.

FINDING FOCUS IN FIRST PRINCIPLES THINKING

Meditation is ultimately a powerful tool for creating focus because it brings clarity of thought. It allows us to stay longer in a single place rather than darting from idea to idea. Our lives today are so overstimulated, both in the real world and through the siren's call of technology, that finding focus requires reaching a sense of clarity, simplicity, and singularity. This is why Ichigyo Zammai becomes such a meaningful practice in daily life. It allows an individual to focus on single tasks and experience them directly. To take an example from mindfulness, you can't be mindful and meditate if you're also texting your friend—you've got to give the task at hand your complete focus and energy.

But you can also clarify and improve your discourse by taking ideas and working them down to their most core components. In social relationships, emotional complexity can lead to misunderstandings. Therefore, agreeing on key foundations is a great way to start a civil discussion. In professional situations, starting from base, core assumptions about your product, brand, audience, or vision allows everyone participating in teamwork to start from the same page. This means not only focusing your own mind but also finding a shared focus by beginning with a clear, simplified set of assumptions. The other thing you should do, then, is define terms for your goals. Search for any word in a dictionary, and you'll likely find that it has multiple definitions. Therefore, to kick off a discussion that's deep or meaningful, define terms so everyone knows exactly what they mean before you move forward.

The best way to accomplish this collaborative focus and this clarification of ideas is to always search for First Principles. A "First Principle" is a core truth: not a conclusion based on models or a pre-supposition based on an expert's opinion. Rather, a First Principle is the simple truth that you come to after you have all extraneous data and are left only with the facts at hand. First Principles Thinking says that you must strip away everything until you reach these core ideas, then you can start building up from there. In this sense, you are able to truly focus on the facts at hand and make the smartest decisions based on the current situation.

More importantly, First Principles Thinking goes hand in hand with civil discourse. By focusing on core truths as a starting point—even as a source of common ground—First Principles Thinking can help focus discourse around accepted truths rather than hotly contested opinions.

The idea that there are First Principles, and that we can try to understand them to serve as the foundation for collaboration and discourse is not remotely new. Aristotle taught his students about the importance of First Causes to shape natural events and chains of consequences. These were called *prime movers*. They only moved on their own and were not moved by other forces. Think of a cat following their favorite sun spot throughout the day. That cat will go where it wants, and good luck trying to get it to move. Both Kant and Descartes, who played with the notion of First Postulates as thinkers during the Enlightenment and translated mathematical and scientific principles to behavioral philosophy.

But today, you are far more likely to hear references to First Principles Thinking from tech titans like Elon Musk and Peter Thiel. By choosing to focus on core truths about their products, their customers, and the future, many top tech innovators are able to translate this mathematical and philosophical principle into a way to make more calculated risks and tackle greater challenges. Working from shared First Principles allowed these leaders to take teams to unprecedented levels, focusing them on common goals and giving them a common vocabulary to encourage productive discourse.

You might question First Principles and find it incredibly difficult to figure out what they are on a given topic you're going to discuss. But the answer to this approach to thinking lies in discourse itself. The best way to boil down situations into their First Principles is to ask questions like:

- Why is this happening?
- What chain of events led to this result?
- Can we clarify this language more simply?
- What would be the consequences of that, and what effects come from that decision?
- Why do we think this is true?
- Where did this assumption come from?
- What was the initial goal/purpose of this line of action?
- What would be an alternative way to view this?

In fact, if you would like to get a master class in First Principles Thinking, take a five-year-old to a science museum. They'll likely ask a slew of interesting questions that you won't know the answer to: *"Why do some dinosaurs eat other dinosaurs and some eat trees?" "Why are some rocks harder than other rocks?" "Why do spiders have eight legs?" "Why can't I have three ice cream cones in one day?"* Children are constantly asking why, in layers upon layers upon layers, again and again. They don't just stop with the first question. They keep asking until they reach a satisfying core truth that cannot be broken down to a smaller reason—or until they've fallen asleep in the car on the way home. Even when you go deeper into answering a question for a child, they'll likely ask "why" to go even further. Sometimes, I'm sure, they do this because they want an answer that can satiate their natural curiosity. Other times, they may be asking "why" to test the boundaries. How annoyed can they get you—and how much mindfulness meditation will you need to counter it?

Either way, the five-year-old's impulse is the natural, unhindered wonderment and curiosity that leads them to search for First Principles. And while anyone who has spent an afternoon with a five-year-old can tell you that asking "but why?" is one of the more annoying habits of young children, it is perhaps also one of the most admirable: they never stop asking fundamental questions, and they never stop trying to gain a clearer understanding of the world around them.

Somewhere, between our youth and adulthood, we are discouraged from constantly asking "why?" Sometimes we adopt an attitude that just accepts the world as it is and assumes our thinking as correct. But that's the wrong attitude! The moment we stop asking "why?" is the moment we stop growing. Still, the best and brightest of us ignore the aspect of society that tells us to dampen our curiosity. By harnessing the mindset of the curious child, we can continue to ask "why" again and again. That is First Principles Thinking.

So, First Principles Thinking not only helps us find the focus we need to have productive discourse. If done properly, the very process of searching for First Principles can itself be a meaningful, civil discussion. This is why adopting First Principles Thinking offers opportunities for growth and improvement of civil discourse at multiple levels: it provides clarity of thought while also creating an opportunity to share ideas and reach a joint consensus.

First Principles Thinking
QUESTIONS AND ANSWERS

Q: Won't other people be annoyed that I'm always asking why?

A: Probably! Asking smart and pointed questions rather than just asking "why?" goes a long way in ensuring you won't sound exactly like an obnoxious five-year-old. As is the case with all discourse, your tone and your active listening skills will help people understand why you are always asking for clarification. And having the reputation as the person who asks a lot of questions is certainly far better than having the reputation as the person who makes ill-informed arguments and never probes further.

I will also say from personal experience that the executives at my companies who I respect the most are the ones who engage in First Principles Thinking. They are always asking "why?" and are not afraid to pause collaboration to bring the team back to a core truth if necessary. They are not afraid to ask unpleasant questions to make conversations more productive, and they play an integral role in providing focus and clarity during group discussions.

Some questions you could ask with First Principles Thinking while remaining respectful could be:

- Why do you think this is the best way to go about it (the topic)?

- What are the benefits and risks of what you're saying?

- Why does it have to work that way?

- Do you have other ideas that you've considered that weren't as productive as what you're proposing? What were they?

SUMMARY

For some, maintaining focus is much easier said than done. Everybody struggles with it from time to time, especially when there are a thousand technological stimuli fighting for your attention. It's especially hard if you have multiple kids running around, demanding that you do everything from show them how to use the TV to make them a cheese sandwich. Despite humanity's struggles with focusing, some of the best practices to enhance and maintain concentration have been around for centuries. By practicing Ichigyo Zammai and mindfulness meditation, you can increase your ability to focus and avoid distractions. At the same time, aiming for civil discourse can ensure that you keep your mind focused on finding truth and mutually beneficial results as often as possible.

When working to maintain or improve your ability to focus, just remember:

- Focusing is not an innate skill. It must be practiced and cultivated. By clearing your mind and focusing on little tasks as you do them, you can strengthen your ability to focus on more important tasks or conversations as they arise.
- Be patient; maintaining focus takes a lot of practice and concentration. Don't expect immediate change.
- Even if you find mindfulness meditation to be difficult, stick with it. This ancient practice is one of the best ways to help you have greater self-awareness and anchor in the present moment.
- Always stay curious and utilize First Principles Thinking to ground you in core truths that can serve as the foundation of any civil discussion.
- Focusing on and prioritizing civil discourse ensures that you don't miss great opportunities to learn and grow with others.

FINAL QUESTIONS AND ANSWERS

Q: What steps can I personally take to focus on civil discourse in my daily life?

A: Focusing on civil discourse requires that you take the necessary steps to simply converse with others in a productive, respectful, and meaningful way. You don't have to organize group debates on ways to save the planet (although you certainly can); you just have to make civil discourse a regular part of your life. Like drinking water or engaging in hobbies, work to make civil discourse something that you actively do as often as possible. It's as easy as pivoting a conversation in a way that minimizes the chance of unproductive arguing and maximizes the collective ability to learn and grow.

Q: What should I do if I am focused, but other people are not?

A: This is a common situation. You start a conversation with someone and you intend to engage with them genuinely, but they are just scrolling on their phone or preoccupied with something else. Just because you are focused does not mean that everyone else will be. Sometimes, you may need to make the conversation more interesting for the other participant. Ask them questions that require them to engage with you. Perhaps try to find a First Principle you can agree on as a focal point to start. If they are still not willing to focus, you may just need to step away and try again another time.

However, you can also get direct with people. You can ask them politely if they can put their phones away while you have a conversation. Perhaps they're trying to send a text or email they really need to send, and you can give them the space to finish that off before you have that discussion. Perhaps they just value their phone more than you because you can't compete with a video of a chihuahua going down a slide (can anyone?). In that case, watch the video together and discuss!

Part Three
Overcoming Challenges

Chapter Eight
Seeking Common Ground

My parents got divorced when I was nine years old. I probably don't have to tell you that it was difficult for me. Although it was devastating, I feel like it was probably inevitable. My father had an affair with someone (who he's now married to), which was the final indication that the marriage was going to end. Any breakup involves multiple communication breakdowns.

For my sister and me, it felt like living in a war zone. We were like soldiers being transported back and forth between the front lines.

Three days at Mom's.

Four days at Dad's.

Four days at Mom's.

Three days at Dad's.

Repeat.

The tension was high. And there was someone else involved, someone not part of the family.

My dad's new partner, in my nine-year-old eyes, was the wedge that had come between my parents. She was the reason my family had been torn in two. In reality, my father owns much of the blame to this day. This story is not one unfamiliar to many children across America, with divorce holding a steady success rate in splitting unions.

There wasn't much my sister and I, at ages eleven and nine, could do except maybe borrow a few ideas from film. We could *Parent Trap* her.

It started small at first. We would ignore her when she said, "Hi," to us. We would refuse to look her in the eye. If it was awkward enough, maybe she would leave. Then, my dad would have no choice but to get back together with my mom, right?

Wrong. Simply ignoring her didn't work, so my sister and I would have to channel our inner demons. Nothing was safe—from her clothes to her eardrums—we were on a mission.

To our dismay, though, real life did not reflect the movies. In fact, she and my dad are happily married today.

Though it took me a little while, eventually my stepmom and I did find some common ground: we both loved my father.

My stepmother and I have grown to form a civil relationship, one built on understanding and a recognition that we have a lot more in common than we initially realized. We want what's best for my dad, so we act like adults, which means I no longer pretend she doesn't exist.

Revenge is an impulse not suited for civil discourse.

Typically, conflicts arise when no common ground can be found between groups or individuals in conversations. Whether the situation involves two classmates who cannot agree on how to finish a group project or two nations on the brink of war, common ground is key to reaching any kind of peaceful, productive resolution. Or, at the very least, common ground allows the conversation to move away from antagonism and toward collaboration.

Each of us have common ground on which we stand, and I'm not just talking about the fact we must all comply with gravity and stand on the earth we share (except, sometimes, for astronauts, I guess). We each have to breathe, sleep, eat, drink, look after, or interact with families and friends—and much more.

Fortunately, because we share some biological and cultural realities, we all have the shared quality of the human experience and are privy to the delights and perils of the human condition. Though it may sound naive, the reality is that humans relate to one another at very basic emotional and rational levels. We all share common ground. From this starting point, you can navigate to a place where all parties are focused more on the benefits of their common ground than prejudices or perceived drawbacks of their differences.

THE HUMAN CONNECTION

What is it about humans that makes us feel connected to one another? How can we know if these connections are real or mere reflections of our upbringing and social environment? If human connections are real and important, what can we do to foster these connections and build on them to find more common ground with others? In this section, I will answer each of these questions to the best of my ability, with the help of scientific research and real-world examples.

First, I want to make it clear that we are, by nature, social animals. We understand ourselves, not just as individuals, but in our social relationships to other people. Back when we lived in more hunter-gatherer societies, it was especially important to be reciprocating, and we have a built-in biological drive we call "tit-for-tat." Essentially, when we do something kind for someone, we naturally feel good about it.

Back in the day, if one of our ancestors (Fred) were to share meat in the winter with someone (Barney) who had none, tit-for-tat thinking would mean that if Fred got hungry the next winter, Barney would be more likely to return the favor. Reciprocation, therefore, was likely a survival technique.

So what makes you feel connected to other human beings? First, it is important to point out that this is not an exclusively human trait. There have been various studies showing that different species of animals have the capacity to show affection and empathetic behavior toward others—particularly members of their own tribe. Chickens, fish, mice, apes, elephants, and dozens of other animal species have all shown the ability to want to protect other animals from danger, give up their own resources to help other animals in need, and go to great lengths to demonstrate empathy. Again, this is likely a survival technique. The more members of the tribe thrive, the higher chance that *you'll* thrive.

If you have ever had a pet, you probably know that interspecies empathy is not uncommon, either. Have you ever looked into a dog's eyes and felt that there was a caring, empathetic creature looking back at you? That's because many animals, particularly those that have evolved to live among humans, have the propensity to show what we might call "love" for their caretakers. Brain scans of dogs have shown that the parts of the brain associated with love, affection, and empathy light up whenever they see their owners or other animals that they like. In fact, it's commonly understood that when your dog puts their paw over your arm, especially when you are petting them, they are essentially petting you back (though maybe they could put in more effort than a limp paw). In short, we are not unique in our ability to be empathetic; we just have a capacity to express and communicate our empathy in more complex ways.

While we as humans may not be the sole arbiters of empathy in existence, we have evolved to communicate our connection with one another in ways that are far more advanced than any other species we have encountered. Not only can we communicate through facial expressions, body language, and actions, but we can use extremely advanced languages—using our voices to form speech, and our hands and fingers to write words—that have evolved over centuries of human interaction. Thus, empathy—and our ability to express empathy in thousands of different ways—form the basis of the human connection.

Blues musician, author, and activist Daryl Davis is one of the greatest examples of setting aside differences, striving to find common ground, and making empathetic, human connections even when the cards were stacked against him. In 2016, a documentary entitled *Accidental Courtesy: Daryl Davis, Race & America* highlighted the story of Davis, an African-American man who spent more than thirty years getting to know members of the Ku Klux Klan. Since beginning his journey to know and even befriend members of the infamous hate group, Daryl Davis has helped more than 200 members leave the KKK for good.

When Davis was just ten years old, he joined an all-White Cub Scouts group and was struck by rocks and bottles during a public march. The incident confused Davis at the time, but it also established his lifelong interest in the origins of racism and racist aggression toward others. Years later, while performing at a bar, a White man approached Davis and complimented him on his musical abilities. After speaking with each other for a while, the man confessed that he had never sat down to have a drink with a Black man before. Shortly thereafter, he admitted that he was a card-carrying member of the Ku Klux Klan. It was this chance encounter that inspired Daryl Davis to seek out other members of the KKK.

When recounting this first discussion with a KKK member, Davis explained why he chose not to just walk away after learning about the stranger's affiliation with the hate group:

> He was very friendly, it was the music that brought us
> together. He wanted me to call him and let him know any-
> time I was to return to this bar with this band. The fact that a
> Klansman and Black person could sit down at the same table
> and enjoy the same music, that was a seed planted. So what
> do you do when you plant a seed? You nourish it. That was the
> impetus for me to write a book. I decided to go around the
> country and sit down with Klan leaders and Klan members
> to find out: How can you hate me when you don't even know
> me?[20]

Thus began Davis's decades-long journey to discover the roots of racism in America. He spent a great deal of time studying the Klan and its ideologies so that he could enter discussions with the greatest weapon of all—knowledge. More often than not, his efforts to understand their beliefs helped build a sense of trust among the KKK members Davis met. By spending time developing a better understanding of how to communicate with those we fundamentally abhor, Davis was able to build up enough trust to have return visits and really get to know individual members. These return visits made it much easier for Davis to expand the conversations, find common ground, and break down the racial divide—as well as the attitudes and beliefs of the KKK members that separated them:

> [It] began to chip away at their ideology, because when two enemies are talking, they're not fighting. It's when the talking ceases that the ground becomes fertile for violence. If you spend five minutes with your worst enemy—it doesn't have to be about race, it could be about anything . . . you will find that you both have something in common. As you build upon those commonalities, you're forming a relationship and as you build about that relationship, you're forming a friendship. That's what would happen. I didn't convert anybody. They saw the light and converted themselves.[21]

It may be difficult to see beyond differences but pushing yourself to broaden your inner circle . . . by extending your trust, expanding your empathy, and talking . . . to people with vastly different backgrounds than you—whether it be race, socioeconomic status, educational background, sexuality, or anything else—is what makes the human capacity for interpersonal connections unique. We can make conscious decisions to overlook differences or, better yet, discuss our differences to gain a better understanding of people outside our trusted communities. More often than not, this allows us to form human connections based on our most fundamental shared traits.

If you are like nearly every other human on the planet, you want to be loved, accepted, appreciated, and respected. Talking with others, asking questions, listening intently, and seeing people as people—your equal and fellow human beings (rather than adversaries or things of lesser value)—can all help you develop a more open mind and understand what it means to share your human identity with billions of other people.

The Human Connection
QUESTIONS AND ANSWERS

Q: What do you mean by "the human connection?"

A: When I say "the human connection," I mean the basic sense of relatedness we feel with other people. When you see a cat or a dog you may have positive emotions and empathy, but there is a special type of connection that humans can feel for one another because we all have the same basic experiences. We all are born, we all have certain hopes and dreams, we all have the knowledge that one day we will die—and the list goes on and on. These basic traits and indisputable facts make our brains react differently to humans than we do to other species. Moreover, our ability to communicate with humans is far more advanced, allowing us to develop even deeper connections based on shared experiences and complex thought processes.

EXPLORING EMPATHY

Davis's story shows us that with dedicated effort, we can empathize with others and encourage them to empathize with us. Davis accomplished this in part through direct connection and personal rapport with others. But we know it is also possible to feel empathy for those who we never meet and who we may not even have any direct connection with.

One way that we see such empathy pursued is through the practice of dark tourism, which is when people travel to sites of great human tragedy in order to learn from the stories and histories of those who experience it. Across Central and Eastern Europe, several sites of Nazi atrocity are open to the public as educational centers. Even in the United States, the Freedom Tower stands as a memorial and educational center where we can feel an empathetic connection with those who lost their lives on 9/11. In each case, visitors are seeking to experience empathy with individuals they have never met—many of whom came from entirely different cultures or societies.

An exceptional example of this phenomenon can be found in America's capital: the National Holocaust Museum in Washington, DC. This educational facility helps visitors understand and place into context the horrors of the Holocaust. When visitors arrive, they are given the copy of an identification document of a real victim in the Holocaust. As the visitor progresses through the exhibits, they learn more about the individual journey of their assigned victim. Many visitors discover that the person they get to know did not survive the Holocaust, allowing the guest to empathize with the victims of Nazi violence. Rather than experiencing the museum in a distant and disconnected manner, the visitor is able to directly empathize with victims and better engage in the difficult civil discourse necessary to process the lessons learned from the exhibits. By creating a situation where visitors can empathize with victims, the curators of the National Holocaust Museum have prepared an excellent environment for civil discourse.

As social creatures, we are inclined to form emotional bonds with others, which is often a precursor to feelings of sincere empathy—even if we do not have direct contact with those people. That is why dark tourism and sites like the National Holocaust Museum can create a feeling of empathy, even for individuals distant in time and space. While it may not be visible in some people, the vast majority of human beings have the natural capacity to express empathy for one another and even go out of their way to help others. This is the first step toward finding common ground and building on the fundamental human connection.

Exploring Empathy
QUESTIONS AND ANSWERS

Q: I'm not a naturally empathetic person. Is there something wrong with me?

A: No, even if you don't have much empathy for other people, this doesn't mean that there is something wrong with you. Everyone's brain is wired a little differently. Besides, empathy doesn't have to be something highly emotional. You can also find a rational stance to build a different kind of empathy for others. You might see that someone else has a broken leg, and you remember the pain you felt at a time when you broke a bone. Though you might not feel strong feelings of sympathy or empathy for the person, you can still use reason to surmise that they understand a type of pain that you also understand. In doing so, you can begin to form a connection with the person through mutual experience.

Q: I empathize with those close to me, but I find it difficult to empathize with strangers. Can I still find common ground with them?

A: This is actually extremely common. People have a tendency to feel much closer and more empathetic toward people from their own "tribe." This applies in a wide range of sociological spheres—from your nationality and political affiliation to sexuality and gender identity. It is especially strong for those who are closest to you, in what you might call your "inner circle": family members, friends, and coworkers. However, distant acquaintances, complete strangers, and people from other "tribes" will likely receive less empathy or compassion from you. This is at the very core of why people feel more comfortable in their echo chambers and why discourse can become so contentious when our tribe is challenged.

Fortunately, lacking empathy from strangers is often a direct result of lacking trust in those you do not know well, and that is a challenge that can be addressed. As I have discussed in previous chapters, you can extend trust to others for the sake of civil discourse, which means that you can also extend a certain degree of trust to strangers to allow empathy to come about more naturally. Unsurprisingly, conversing and getting to know someone will allow you to understand them a little bit more—even if you still consider them to be a "stranger." This, in turn, will help you find common ground and overcome the difficulty of trusting and empathizing with people outside your inner circle.

LOOKING FOR COMMONALITY

For most people, simply being a member of the same species or occupying the same planet is not enough to reach out and find common ground. Differences of age, gender, ethnicity, socioeconomic background, political affiliation, and a thousand other factors can all affect our desire to find commonality. This is why it is so important to start at the basics. In most discussions, people start from their biggest differences and attempt to debate. More often than not, this results in participants aiming to defeat their opponent because they have entered the conversation focused on seemingly irreconcilable differences.

Many people want to skip past the "getting to know you" phase and go straight into the deep, often-controversial topics. I probably don't need to provide evidence for you to know that "What's your stance on abortion?" is not as good an introductory question as "So what do you do?" or "Where are you from?" Not only is a controversial question a little off-putting, but it also frames the discussion in a way that feels inherently adversarial. If you are asking that question to begin a discussion, you are likely trying to determine if someone is in your tribe or not. Are they a friend or foe? Are they a good person or a bad person? Do they deserve your respect or your contempt?

Instead, I encourage people to start interactions with basic points of commonality. This can be done by asking questions to get to know the other person. Find out about their interests, hobbies, background, and so on. At some point, you will find something that you have in common. The human connection is already a given, but getting beyond the basic experiences of human life is often the best way to find common ground and work to build a respectful dialogue. So if the other person jumps into a heavier topic, try to steer them back to starting with a commonality you have together.

This is not to say that you can't or shouldn't talk about differences. In fact, talking about differences is essential for civil discourse. However, many discussions are derailed because they start with major differences and have nowhere positive to go from there. Both participants are more likely to dig in their heels, stick to their guns, and lose more and more respect for the other with each passing second.

The way that you reach people is by separating ideas from identity and beginning discourse with the intention of finding common ground. The first, most indirect approach to finding commonality is to ask for objective information or a subjective viewpoint. These can be real and crucial questions that require conversing with a stranger or someone you may be at odds with. It doesn't matter if the person you're asking knows the answer; it's merely a method to start a conversation. It doesn't even matter if you don't know the answer:

"Do you know where the nearest Starbucks is located?"

"Excuse me, but do you know when the speeches start?"

"Do you like the food here?"

"What were your thoughts on the panel discussion?"

The first two instances seek objective knowledge, but the last two want a subjective judgment. The second approach to finding common ground is to comment on something you both have in common. "Why are you both at your friend's place?"

"What brings you both to this networking event in Tallahassee?"

"What unfortunate event drove you to the DMV this morning?"

"So who do you know around here? So how did you meet Jack?"

"Have you asked Jack about the time he went skiing with his dog?"

The idea behind these similarities is that they are quick discussion starters. There is a clear answer behind them.

Look for elements of yourself in others. What do you share with them in this moment or in life? If you have differences, are they differences that cause friction? If so, why do they cause friction? Is there a way that you can overcome these differences? Frequently, starting from a point of commonality and working toward more complex or controversial topics is a much more effective strategy for engaging in civil discourse.

Looking for Commonality
QUESTIONS AND ANSWERS

Q: How can I look for commonality without seeming intrusive?

A: When it comes to discussions and civil discourse, context is everything. In most cases, you can start with broad questions that are unlikely to be misinterpreted. Asking about people's personal interests and hobbies are almost always safe territory (unless their hobby is putting pineapple on pizza). From there, you can break the ice further by discussing your own interests. Ideally, you and the other person will find one or more points of commonality. This opens the door to discuss more divisive topics in a respectful, productive way.

Q: How can I encourage someone to look for commonality with me?

A: Remember when we talked about self-reflection? It's worth taking some time during that process to reflect on some of your favorite traits, interests, and ways that you easily connect with others. Have answers to simple "getting to know you" kinds of questions in your head so that you can readily connect with someone else who is looking for commonality with you. Think of ideas and interests that you feel confident talking about and use them to open up conversations with others. By reflecting on how you can be a good partner in conversation, you can leave yourself open to someone else finding commonality with you and making the connection.

FINDING CONNECTION THROUGH HUMOR

Making connections and finding common ground can often be done by sharing one of the most universal human experiences: humor. This was a lesson I actually learned from my friend, Iranian American stand-up comedian Max Amini. He continually engages in a dialogue about the power of comedy to spur discourse and discuss socially sensitive issues.

Max and I originally connected over our shared cultural experience, not simply as Iranians, but as Iranian American children of immigrants. Just as many immigrants have shared experiences of nostalgia for their homeland or anxiety over moving somewhere new, the children of immigrants also face their own unique challenges. This includes trying to balance American culture with the values their parents still hold, working to create an identity that bridges two worlds, and struggling with judgment, misunderstanding, or hostility from the society around them. The children of immigrants often struggle to find common ground with others because they cannot fully identify with either their American identity or their parents' cultural identity. Both Max and I expressed frustration with our Iranian identity as teens just like many children of immigrants do.

But as Max and I enjoyed conversations about politics, philosophy, or ethics, we were always able to find common ground in the
ways that we had taken our Iranian American identities and converted them into communication. Max embraced stand-up comedy
often with deeply political messages—utilizing an art form that is
essentially banned in Iran. I initially made my move into writing
online by authoring articles about growing saffron hydroponically,
putting a modern technological spin on the most stereotypical Persian spice one could taste. He and I were able to find common ground
in those experiences of reimagining our Persian identities and then
engage in civil discourse even when our views differed politically,
economically, or socially.

> You know this is really evident that we are a proud culture, Ira-
> nians . . . My American friends say, "What is it about you guys?
> You have so much confidence!"
>
> I tell them, "I've figured it out." It's because of the way our
> mothers raised us . . . from the time we were a baby. It was spe-
> cial. . . . We're the only culture that, when the baby is born, the
> mother will drop the baby up and down and say, "Dodool tala,
> dodool tala, doodol tala!" It's an amazing thing! . . . It means
> "golden dick!" Imagine the confidence that's built with such an
> incredible repetition of positivity![22]
>
> —Max Amini

In fact, one of the most important lessons Max taught me is just
how vital humor can be in civil discourse. While civility and focus
may often lend a seriousness to a conversation that can even create
tension: humor is the remedy that keeps a conversation friendly

and reminds everyone involved that they are starting from a place of common ground. In itself, comedy is a recognition that we both have shared some experience in that *"don't you just hate it when"* sense when everyone can relate to some frustrating, or serendipitous, or absurd experience. Humor can be used to bring everyone back to a shared space of civility and human connection.

So for Max Amini and me, conversations initially blossomed over the common ground we found as the children of immigrants—turning our Iranian American identity into an opportunity for discourse. Over time, I was able to learn the importance of humor in finding that common ground in the first place—both for ourselves and within our expressive art forms. Comedy can be used by anyone to find common ground with others. Using comedy to lighten tense situations and simultaneously bring everyone together can be a powerful way to keep discourse civil, productive, and enjoyable.

Finding Connection Through Humor Discourse
QUESTIONS AND ANSWERS

Q: What are some ways I can use humor to improve discourse in my life?

A: Humor is a great way to break down barriers between people, create common ground, and jump-start trust between you and the person you're speaking with. Adding a humorous ice-breaking activity or conversation to the start of many important discussions can quickly create an initial shared laugh that serves as the foundation for the common ground of civil discourse.

Q: How do I use humor in discourse without turning the conversation into a joke?

A: Remember, while it is important to make human connections and find common ground with someone in order to engage in discourse, that is a mechanism to improve your tone and rapport. You are not making jokes about the topics you are discussing but rather using humor to break the ice or relieve tensions between people you are talking with. Try using different tones when bonding over jokes and actually discussing serious discourse. It is possible to switch between humorous topics and serious topics without making light of the discourse at hand.

Think of it like this; when discussing a topic with someone, humor has different functions depending on the circumstance and the delivery of the joke or lighthearted comment. You can use humor to add a lightness of touch to a situation. Sometimes, if things get too serious, you can use a joke, make everyone smile, and carry on. This is certainly a skill you can cultivate. Since sometimes people use humor as a defense mechanism to obfuscate what they are talking about rather than help alleviate the tension, make sure you're not just poking fun at someone for being vulnerable—like if you know it will probably offend them. Different people have different thresholds and boundaries for humor, so it's best to work these out by staying safe initially and see what is appropriate for the individual(s) you're with or situation you're in.

SUMMARY

At a time when diversity is often hailed as the key to progress, we often forget to find ways in which we are similar. By focusing on differences first, many people develop unnecessary and unjustified biases. This makes it harder to see other people as equals and human beings who deserve as much respect as you do. Fortunately, by focusing on developing empathy for others, working to break out of your "inner circle," recognizing the human connection, and pursuing further points of commonality, you can find common ground with anyone. In short, start with conversing about similarities, then you can work on discussing your differences.

When working to find common ground, just remember:

- People have unique traits, opinions, and beliefs that are very different from yours—and that's okay. Don't act like everyone you speak to will share your point of view; otherwise, you won't give the other person space to share theirs. You shouldn't be afraid of differences, but you also shouldn't let differences dominate your view of others.
- The human connection is just the starting point. Seek to really understand other people on a deeper level, and you will find common ground.

- Don't be afraid to use humor—but not overly cynical or inconsiderate sarcasm—to make connections with others and to find common ground over shared challenges. Gentle, self-deprecating humor can be a great way to break the ice.
- Try to expand your inner circle to include more people who may think, look, speak, or act differently from you.
- Don't let the modern world's state of polarization scare you away from trusting and empathizing with others. At the end of the day, nearly all of us want the same things in life and have the capacity to connect with others.

FINAL QUESTIONS AND ANSWERS

Q: What if I literally have nothing in common with someone?

A: If you are speaking with another human being, you always have something in common (i.e., the human connection). You both breathe oxygen into your lungs after all, and each of you have an unbroken ancestral lineage that reaches all the way back to our common ancestor. However, with some people, you may have to work harder to find more common ground—you can't just talk about how "great that oxygen tastes today!" or ask how great-great-great-great-great-great-great-great-grandma cavewoman is doing. If you can't find any commonality, it is usually a lack of communication that is causing the issue. Failing to ask enough questions or listen attentively might make you believe that you are talking to someone with whom you have no common ground. Just continue to converse respectfully, and you will certainly find commonality.

Q: What can I do if someone is not embracing my attempts to find common ground?

A: Some people may be more than happy to ignore the common ground they share with you. This can make discourse less civil. However, facts are facts. If someone does not want to recognize points of commonality, you can always return to the basics. Remind them that you are just two people conversing. You share the human connection. It might be difficult to convince some people to embrace similarities and be fully aware that you share common ground, but few people can ignore that you are both human beings.

Chapter Nine
Expecting Conflict in Perspectives

I know I've written a whole book on discourse, but discourse was not always my strong suit. When I was younger, I questioned *everything*. And while questioning is good, I wouldn't say I always had the best approach. When I was in middle school, my parents enrolled me in a Catholic school. It was the kind of environment where you were talked *at* rather than talked *to*. We were told exactly what to think and how to think it.

But I was raised with a different tradition. I didn't view what was written in the Bible and how my Catholic school interpreted it as *the* truth. Some things didn't make sense to me, like the idea of God being *everywhere*. Everywhere, really? "If God is everywhere," I asked one day, "does that mean he's in your intestines?" This made the rest of the class laugh. I remember the teacher glaring at me over her glasses, then sending me out of the classroom.

It made no sense to me at the time. Why weren't we allowed to ask questions, especially on issues as important as *God*? Nearly every religion or belief system has a vastly different opinion on what all-powerful force controls the universe, so shouldn't *everyone* be questioning what their religious leaders are telling them? I graduated from the Catholic school feeling like I had been freed from sermonizing, and many memories of it make me feel grateful for the experiences I have had with nonreligious education. Maybe we were only children at the Catholic school, but how were we ever supposed to become prepared for the wider world if we couldn't question what was presented to us as truth?

There's a difference between handling conflicting perspectives gracefully and resorting to uncivil discourse (or, in my case, a trip to the principal who still wouldn't tell me if God was in my intestines). The goal is not avoiding conflict but handling conflicting perspectives productively by utilizing them as an opportunity for civil discourse and the sharing of ideas.

In nearly every instance of civil discourse, there is a necessary element of conflict. I don't mean to imply that civil discourse fundamentally depends on quarreling or antagonism but rather on conflicting ideas and perspectives. Without this type of conflict, civil discourse would be little more than two people constantly agreeing with one another. Unfortunately, this is often what happens when people remain in their ideological bubbles and refuse to reach out to those with different views from their own. Expecting conflicting perspectives and preparing yourself for what civil conflict looks like can ensure that you actually engage in successful discourse and walk away bettered by the experience.

EXAMINING PERSPECTIVE

In the public sphere, we often throw around the word *perspective* without much concern for what the term really means. By default, perspective implies a position of difference. In human terms, perspective is a natural result of subjectivity. We each have our own viewpoint from which we can examine the world around us and form opinions. The collective opinions and observations of one person constitutes their perspective. Consequently, perspective is wholly unique to every individual on the planet.

Even if you find someone who seems to share your opinions on nearly every subject, they still have a unique perspective. They see you (and the rest of the world) from a different vantage point than you see them and everyone else. So, eventually, if you talk with another person for long enough, you will reach a conflict of perspectives. These conflicts can be as inconsequential as differences in visual perspectives (looking at the same object from different vantage points) to conflicting perspectives on the existence of a higher power. Accepting differing perspectives as a natural part of human experience is necessary so that you can open your mind to different ideas, opinions, and intellectual positions.

Social media and the Internet at large provide us some of the best examples of conflicting perspectives on a massive scale. Posts, videos, and images that go viral often do so because they bring out our differences in perspective very quickly. In 2015, a picture of a seemingly normal dress had people falling into two opposing camps based on their unique perspectives. Some people argued vehemently that the dress was white and gold while others argued that it was black and blue. Despite its lack of importance in the grand scheme of things, it became a topic of heated debate both online and off. Mainstream news outlets picked up the story to debate how and why the whole thing was taking place.

Even academia began to weigh in as the issue brought about questions regarding the basic characteristics of our visual experiences and how much of our world is a result of genuine data outside our heads versus how much of it is structured internally. Pascal Wallisch, clinical assistant professor of psychology at New York University, had this to say about the infamous dress phenomenon:

> Even outside of vision scientists, most people just assume everyone sees the world in the same way. Which is why it's awkward when disagreements arise—it suggests one party either is ignorant, is malicious, has an agenda, or is crazy. We believe what we see with our own eyes more than almost anything else, which may explain the feuds that occurred when "the dress" first struck and science lacked a clear explanation for what was happening.[23]

After people got tired of arguing about a seemingly random and insignificant topic, science finally offered a few answers that helped explain what had happened in 2015. According to Wallisch, "people's perspective of color is also informed by their perspective of lighting . . . it is well-known that in situations like this—where [the brain] faces profound uncertainty—it confidently fills in the gaps in knowledge by making assumptions."[24] As a result, millions of people saw different color combinations based on their perspective of the lighting in the photo and their brain's inherent desire to understand external stimuli, even when there was insufficient or conflicting information.

This is just one example of people interpreting images in different ways—something that happens all the time in the art world. Why would film critics, music critics, or any kind of art critics exist if everyone viewed and interpreted films, songs, paintings, or other artistic endeavors in the same way? The truth is that they wouldn't. We are not all robots with the exact same programming. We are individual beings with our own ways of absorbing and evaluating new information. Also, our brain makes up the majority of our perceptions despite being influenced by external stimuli. Even the lens of our eyes projects an upside-down, two-dimensional image onto our retina, which our brain flips into a right-side-up, three-dimensional image.

Looking back to early thought, Aristotle was one of the first philosophers to openly embrace the idea that human beings each have individual perspectives that are based on their subjective experiences. This stood in stark contrast to many of the prevailing beliefs of the day. He argued that human nature is not objective and therefore truth can only be known to the degree that our individual subjectivity allows. This means that, in Aristotle's view, objective reality or objective knowledge only exists through individual sense experience.

While I personally believe in an objective reality—one that exists almost entirely outside human perception—Aristotle made a compelling point. How can we have confidence in the existence of an objective reality when we only have our own subjectivity to rely on? This question begs a thousand more inquiries on the nature of our existence, but it also reinforces the importance of collaboration through civil discourse.

Just think about it. As an individual human with your own perspective of existence, the best way to learn, grow, and expand your worldview is to expose yourself to differing perspectives. This is why living in an intellectual "bubble"—consistently inside our own heads and not dialoguing enough with others to get an indication of what goes on in theirs—is antithetical to growth and self-improvement. We need the perspectives of others to enhance our understanding of the world around us.

Examining Perspective
QUESTIONS AND ANSWERS

Q: What is the difference between subjectivity and perspective?

A: A lot of people may think that there's little or no difference between these two words, but this is only because they are so closely related. For the sake of clarity, it is important to distinguish between the two terms. Subjectivity refers to the quality of existing within the mind of an individual as opposed to the external world that we perceive. Perspective, on the other hand, is simply a point of view. Therefore, perspective falls under the umbrella of subjectivity, but the two are still distinct. Subjectivity relates to the general experience of being an individual while perspective relates to the specific views and opinions that arise from living a subjective experience.

Q: If everyone has different perspectives, how can we hope to find the truth?

A: It has long been the belief that humans, on many subjects, cannot find objective truth. However, we can always move closer to the truth simply by pursuing it. We may go in the wrong direction at times, but the mere pursuit of truth and the desire to know the truth ensure that we can get closer to knowing what is true and what is false. Trying to find the truth just by thinking and limiting yourself to your own perspective is nearly impossible. We all need to accept that we don't know everything and can learn something from everyone, thereby moving us closer to the truth together.

Q: Will anticipating differences really make it easier to engage with conflicting perspectives?

A: Without a doubt! If you assume that someone will agree with some or even all of what you say, you will be far more likely to react with a combative mindset. Instead, you should assume that differences will arise. Be ready to discuss them calmly, even if you feel strongly about the subject matter. Preparing for pushback is like giving yourself an emotional set of armor that will allow you to have a civil discussion.

CONFLICTING PERSPECTIVES ON CAMPUS

As I discussed briefly in the preface, my experience at Colorado College was not the intellectual utopia that I had expected when I showed up fresh-faced and excited for a new challenge. People were not always willing to share their views out of fear of becoming socially denounced or isolated by their peers. Some were worried about experiencing potential retribution from their professors. The majority of public discourse surrounding the stifling of free thought on college campuses has focused on the "liberal slant" of university professors and the ostracization of more right-leaning faculty and students. However, the truth is that students (and many professors) from all parts of the political spectrum feel the need to hesitate before sharing their honest opinions or forgo speaking about controversial topics entirely. Both liberal and conservative voices are stifled to varying degrees at campuses across America today.

Even when professors avoided an outwardly political bent in their teaching, students could often surmise some basic elements of their political thoughts based on how they formed curricula, the parts of the course that they gave greater emphasis, and the topics that they avoided. Since students look to professors as experts in their respective fields and beacons for guidance, many of my classmates would (sometimes subconsciously) find themselves asking and answering questions in a way that they thought would align with the professor's views. Even if it went against their real political beliefs, many students were willing to abandon their principles to win brownie points, stay in the professor's good graces, and avoid causing conflict in the classroom—sometimes even altering how they wrote essays to get a better grade. This is hardly a new phenomenon, indeed.

Naturally, such ass-kissing did not always work. In just about every class there was someone who had very strong convictions and refused to be deterred, even when there was an authority in the room. So on very rare occasions, conflicts in perspective would arise in class discussions. But whenever this did happen, something strange would occur. It was like viewing a psychological thought experiment in real time.

- One student would express an opinion, and another would counter with their own opinion.
- The students would continue to argue until they reached an impasse or the professor would put a stop to it so that they could continue with their lesson plan.
- Students who were not directly involved in the argument would look at the professor to gauge their reaction.
- If the professor showed no preference for one opinion over the other, everyone remained quiet.
- On the other hand, if the professor seemed to support one opinion, even through subtle facial expressions or body language, other students were more likely to join in to support the professor's preferred student and talk down the "dissenter."

It was a weird kind of mob mentality that ebbed and flowed based on—what appeared to me, at least—the subconscious whims of the nearest authority figure. This happened again and again in my classes, from in person to when we moved online. It was like a cycle of silencing in some effort to ensure authority remained pleased.

Outside the classroom, where students didn't have a professor to guide them, they only had their own opinions to rely on. From a social perspective, this was a far more frightening prospect. What if someone disagrees with you? Even worse, what if multiple people disagree with you? What if word spreads that you have unpopular opinions or political views? Will you become the campus pariah?

These are the thoughts that swirl through students' heads every day. The groupthink that often arises from campus culture is not due to some kind of political agenda being enforced on campuses across the country or around the world. It is just the result of people fearing conflict and ostracization in an environment that should foster free thought and open dialogue. People withdraw from expressing opinions because they fear someone will disagree with them. Why start an argument when you can keep your thoughts to yourself and remain socially palatable to everyone? Maybe that's the ultimate, short-term survival technique. But that doesn't exactly create the conditions for people to thrive.

Even if you take away the potential social repercussions of speaking your mind, there is also the fear of defending your position. Research into the political views of teenagers and college-age adults has shown that most fall into one of two categories. On the one hand, there are those who adopt the same (or similar) political views as their parents. On the other hand, there are those who "rebel" and adopt political views that are the polar opposite of their parents. However, this is a bit of an oversimplification for two reasons. First, not all children develop political views based on the views of their parents, and second, not all children can accurately identify the political views of their parents.

In fact, political scientists Christopher Ojeda and Peter K. Hatemi found a connection between understanding political beliefs and bonding between parents and their children:

The transmission of party identification from parent to child is one of the most important components of political socialization in the United States. Research shows that children learn their party identification from their parents, and parents drive the learning process. The vast majority of studies thus treats children as passive recipients of information and assumes that parent-child concordance equals transmission. Rather than relying on a single pathway by which parents teach children, we propose an alternative view by focusing on children as active agents in their socialization. In so doing, we introduce a two-step model of transmission: perception then adoption.[25]

The study found that roughly two-thirds of children were able to accurately perceive their parent's political affiliations. Nearly half of the children who correctly identified their parent's political affiliations adopted their political views while just 18 percent rejected them. Consequently, among all children involved in the study, only one in four children fell into the "politically rebellious" category, even if some of these children did not know their parents' true political beliefs.

So what does all of this have to do with conflicting perspectives on campus? As previously mentioned, fear of social repercussions suppresses political discourse on many college campuses. However, when the political views of parents are the primary indicators of a student's political beliefs entering college, this means that they may engage in debates without having ever properly analyzed why they believe or don't believe in something. They oppose abortion because their parents oppose abortion or they support government reparations for African Americans because their parents support them, too.

Many students enter college with strong convictions and weak arguments because they just haven't given the issues much thought. They are likely more emotionally connected to their views because of affiliation than connected to them through reasoning (although, these things can overlap and go hand in hand). Like the students I surveyed in college classrooms, many children, teens, and young adults prefer to turn to the nearest authority figure and parrot their beliefs without question.

This makes the prospect of conflicting perspectives somewhat frightening. Not only could you lose friends by expressing yourself, but you could look extremely foolish at the same time. Imagine that you proudly proclaim yourself as being fiscally liberal and socially conservative. Perhaps you're not well versed in the ins and outs of the statement made, and it's something you've heard and regurgitated. Perhaps you even have a loose affiliation to the statement. Then, someone starts asking you questions. "So do you support the government nanny state?" "Are you saying you oppose gay marriage?" Suddenly, your unassuming statement of self-identification has embroiled you in a heated debate for which you are ill-prepared. For many college students, it is easier and safer to just shut up and nod along with the crowd, in fear of either being wrong or being shunned socially.

Fortunately, this is where the practice of asking questions serves a much greater purpose. Rather than walking into a room and stating what you believe, start asking about what other people believe. Whether you're one-on-one or in a group, people are more likely to engage positively when you show an interest in their beliefs, even if they have various reasons to feel stifled in a college environment. You don't need to pry or avoid talking about your own opinions, but creating an environment of inquiry is far more likely to produce positive results than simply regurgitating what you, your parents, or your professor believes.

Conflicting Perspectives on Campus
QUESTIONS AND ANSWERS

Q: I'm a college student with different views than most of my peers. How can I express myself without being ridiculed or isolated?

A: Most people fear the social consequences of their beliefs far more than they need to. People will certainly argue with you, but if you express yourself calmly and clearly, the "consequences" will be negligible. That said, it is important that you show respect for others. You cannot express a view that is overtly harmful to an individual or group and expect there to be no repercussions.

If you state that you are a Republican or Democrat, for example, people may challenge your political views, but you can still engage in civil discourse if you focus on collaborative dialogue. However, if you state that one race of people is superior to another, you will likely put yourself in a situation where people are openly hostile and unwilling to listen to your rationale. This is because your view, by default, shows a lack of respect for others at a fundamental level, and at a level that is antagonistic to others. So, if you have controversial views or ostensibly "bad takes," make sure you practice self-reflection and examine your views thoroughly to understand why you believe in them. This process may lead you to have even greater conviction in your beliefs, or it may lead you to abandon them entirely.

Q: I'm a college student who's interested in encouraging civil discourse on campus. What can I do?

A: The best way to encourage civil discourse on campus is to participate in it and create opportunities for others to do so as well. If you belong to student groups, try to put together or sponsor events with experts or guests with opposing viewpoints to show how discourse about difficult topics should play out. Attend talks or events with friends, and then grab dinner and discuss the topic of the talk. Even choosing to write an op-ed in your campus newspaper demonstrating both sides of an issue and encouraging civil discourse is an opportunity to start productive conversations at your school.

INVITING CONFLICTS IN PERSPECTIVE

Thus far, I've been focused on some of the anxiety surrounding conflicts in perspective, which may lead you to believe that differing opinions are something to be avoided. This could not be further from the truth. Getting outside your comfort zone just comes with the territory of engaging in civil discourse. You will often engage with people or ideas that make you uncomfortable. This is where civil discourse lives and thrives: in those gray areas between what is "right" and "wrong."

When you take part in everyday, polite conversations, people usually try to avoid these conflicts. We do this for the sake of propriety but also out of the very human desire to protect ourselves. Differences can lead to conflict, conflict to disdain, disdain to hatred, and hatred to violence. Keeping things civil by subtly evading touchy subjects is simply what humans do to get along and ensure their own survival. It can also be time saving and situationally inappropriate to start a certain type of conversation. If you're in a store you've never been to, is it really necessary to ask a cashier you've never met what they think about *Roe v. Wade*? Despite the rest of your interaction being more polite and transactional, where you have a chance to find common ground and talk about the weather, you're going straight for something that divides opinion. You're spending a few seconds on something that often takes hours to explore.

Furthermore, practicing civil discourse does not mean that you throw all manners and decorum out the window. In fact, it wouldn't be very "civil" if you were shouting your opinions at another person, nor would it be proper discourse. Therefore, rather than trying to stay away from conflicting perspectives, you should invite them. Look for areas where ideas or beliefs diverge and dissect them—but always in a framework of mutual respect and collaboration.

At *The Doe*, we didn't aim to shock or sensationalize what our anonymous contributors wrote, but sometimes stories are inherently shocking. There is no better example than one of our most talked-about and controversial pieces, "Having an Orgasm During Rape: I Believed the Myth and Sought Violent Sex." Sexual violence and its prevalence in society are already difficult topics for many people—especially survivors of sexual trauma. When you combine issues of violence with pleasure, many societal taboos are touched upon simultaneously.

Sometimes people don't like to open their eyes to reality because they are afraid of the consequences. What if a man hears that women can orgasm during rape and is therefore more compelled to commit acts of sexual violence? Naturally, this was a concern when we first ran the article. Our team would never want to cause pain or distress to anyone directly or indirectly. But we decided that putting our heads in the sand would not solve anything. And, believe it or not, that article led to hundreds of messages and emails from both men and women who had similar experiences with rape. Studies into nonconsensual sex back up the writer's claims that there is a separation between the "biological reaction to a sexual act" and the actual enjoyment of sex. In the end, the article helped many, many people overcome the shame, guilt, and confusion they felt after having similar experiences.

When our editing team agreed to publish the article, we knew that we were inviting conflicts in perspective. In fact, the initial backlash was a little overwhelming. Some people found the article overly graphic while others wondered (as I previously mentioned) if it would only incentivize people to commit more acts of sexual violence. However, for people who actually read the article from start to finish, the consensus was that the author lived through a terrible experience and had found peace by talking about her experiences privately with others and, finally, sharing her story (albeit anonymously) with the world.

Though *The Doe* took on the risk of publishing the article, the author is the true hero of this story. They wrote about something that few people were willing to talk about in a public setting. This ignited a much-needed discourse on the effects of sexual trauma and how it can shape a person's sense of self-worth for life. They helped others join them on a path of healing. Both the author and *The Doe* invited conflicts in perspective, and it brought about some of the most important and profound discourse we've seen since launching the website in 2019.

To be clear, I'm not saying that you should bring up the most controversial or uncomfortable topic you can imagine at your next family dinner. I really don't want Grandma choking on her radishes! What I am saying is that there is far more power in speaking truth and facing reality than staying silent. Avoiding conflict is the easy route, but it will lead you nowhere. Instead, invite conflict. Look for differences of opinion. Ask questions and tell your story. In doing so, you will find that civil discourse can be both productive and cathartic.

Inviting Conflicts in Perspective
QUESTIONS AND ANSWERS

Q: Isn't inviting conflicts in perspective the same as asking for trouble?

A: Remember that the word *civil* is just as important as the word *discourse*. You don't need to incite rage or cause trauma or look for a fight to invite conflicts in perspective. I simply mean that you should look for areas of difference or discord and work to understand them. When you were in grade school and you didn't understand a math equation, you would ask the teacher about it, right? The same holds true in the realm of civil discourse. If you do not understand someone's point of view or two ideas are incongruous with each other, don't shy away from these issues. Embrace differences of opinion in an environment of respect and honesty.

Q: How can inviting conflicting perspectives be cathartic?

A: One of the easiest ways to understand the potential cathartic benefits of conflict is by imagining two very different scenarios. In the first scenario, you are being interviewed for a job you really want. You likely feel tense, nervous, and scrutinized. In the second, you are speaking with your most trusted friend about your thoughts, feelings, hopes, and dreams. The first scenario is a stressful situation where it is difficult to feel like you can simply be yourself. Alternatively, the second scenario is one where you are free to express your innermost opinions.

The further you get into civil discourse, the more it becomes like the second scenario. Speaking honestly with the intention of finding truth or producing mutually beneficial results becomes easier as your trust in the other participant(s) grows. Once you feel comfortable enough to be completely open, not only will the discourse improve, but it will also feel like a weight has been lifted off your shoulders. You will no longer be limited by silence or fear of repercussions. You can simply speak and listen in earnest.

SUMMARY

Conflicts in perspective are a natural part of the human experience. Even before written history, our ancient ancestors were warring over different beliefs and goals—is that woolly mammoth white and gold or black and blue? Today, not much has changed. But our capacity to understand one another has improved with the evolution of our species. Though we may fear backlash in public spaces, we have the power to understand different perspectives and even express ourselves in ways that can help overcome differences without ignoring them.

When expecting or anticipating conflicts, just remember:

• Nobody is going to agree with you 100 percent of the time. You should always expect some degree of conflict because we are all subjective creatures with our own viewpoints and beliefs.

• Fear is a barrier to civil discourse. If you are afraid to express yourself truthfully, you cannot hope to engage in meaningful civil discourse.

• Fear of conflict is often worse than the actual consequences of conflict. Always be respectful, but don't back down from your principles just because someone disagrees with you. Instead, listen and understand how their perspective differs from yours.

• Looking for conflict is very similar to getting outside your "bubble." If you only surround yourself with people who think the same way as you do, you will stifle your intellectual growth.

FINAL QUESTIONS AND ANSWERS

Q: Can I ever fully understand another person's perspective?

A: I will concede that this is a tough question to answer, both from a scientific and a philosophical standpoint. While it is impossible to fully understand someone's subjective experience, you can come to understand their perspective in meaningful ways. Whether or not you can completely understand a different perspective is difficult to say, as each perspective hinges on the subjectivity of the individual. That said, even if you can only understand a fraction of someone's viewpoint, it is worth pursuing that knowledge to broaden your perspective. You can still empathize with them and gain insight into the human experience from where they stand.

Chapter Ten
Avoiding Poor Discourse

"Avoid poor discourse" sounds like a cop-out statement. After all, if open, honest discourse hinges on the exchange of ideas, how can you simply avoid discourse that is unproductive? Wouldn't that avoidance undermine the entire collaborative point of discourse? While there are some gray areas when it comes to picking and choosing the discourses in which you will engage, one has to draw a line between what is collaborative and combative, productive and unproductive, as well as civil and uncivil. In doing so, you can avoid poor discourse without falling into the trap of running away from ideas or people that you do not like.

When I was riding horses, many of the events took me to unfamiliar places. While Silicon Valley was a laid-back, more casual environment, many competitions took place in the South or the Midwest, which was a much more polite environment—usually. I had to work on shifting my discourse, getting used to saying things like "Yes ma'am" and "Yessir." I had to be sure to never complain and show that I was grateful. I'm sure we've all had moments like this—where we had to code switch or shift our communication to avoid conflict or simply fit in.

As you may be able to imagine, I was one of only maybe thirty or so people of color. A vast majority of riders and stable owners were white. I was very aware that I was different, and it shaped how I communicated. I had to converse in a way that showed I was *not* the other, though. I was like *them.* This isn't to say that I had to pretend like my ancestors had come off the Mayflower, but I did have to demonstrate that I was not some foreigner who would cause problems. I had to prove that I fit in there.

I never experienced any overt harm from racism, but it was prevalent nonetheless. Communication was kind of like when you slow down when driving through a rainstorm. I was aware of every action, every word. I was always certain to make sure the conversation stayed on course.

Once, when talking to an Uber driver in Lexington, Kentucky, he asked me, "Where are you from?! You're not one of those *A-rabs,* are you?"

The truth is that I'm not Arab, of course; I'm Iranian. I knew the implication in what he was saying, though. "A-rab." was his way of questioning if I was from the Middle East. In that moment, it wouldn't have been helpful for me to explain that Iran was not, in fact, on the Arabian Peninsula, or that Iran and Saudi Arabia didn't even touch. I'm not sure how helpful it would have been to explain that Iran and the Arabian Peninsula were completely separated by the Persian Gulf. That's because this gentleman wasn't asking if I was from the country known as Saudi Arabia, or another country on the Arabian Peninsula. He wasn't actually asking if I was Arab, he was "othering" me.

I used my context clues to determine that this was not a type of discourse I was interested in having. So I gave him an answer that I hoped he would want to hear: I told him I was from somewhere else, not the Middle East.

I don't like that I felt like I had to lie. It doesn't feel good knowing that I had to, in a way, validate his question and hide the fact that I was Middle Eastern. But I made a judgment call for my own safety. I don't even know if it was the right thing to do. By hiding a part of my identity from this individual, I was showing this man that what he said was okay. I chose to avoid a difficult conversation because it was easier for me in that moment. What if I had explained to him why what he was saying was problematic? What if it had led to a conversation that led to a change in this man's behavior? Sure, it was possible, but it was also possible that he would respond with an insult or something even worse. Healing and rectifying wrongs are good, but that doesn't mean one individual should be expected to solve every problem that comes their way.

That's part of conflict, though, isn't it? There aren't always obvious answers. You don't always know what the right turn is, even after you've made it.

THE DOUBLE-EDGED SWORD OF SOCIAL MEDIA

We all know that social media has culturally and cognitively changed the way we interact with one another as a species. I have friends and acquaintances with whom I do not exchange any personal messages or phone calls; instead, we just like one another's pictures and videos on Instagram from time to time. If it's a really good post, we might even throw a few fire emojis in the comment section. This state of symbolic communication has become so commonplace that we forget how quickly communication has evolved (or, in some cases, devolved) over the past few decades. In years past, talking heads worried that the email or text message could spell ruin for our species. Naturally, this fearmongering had no real foundation, but our preferred forms of communication have quickly become more simplified and less nuanced, particularly with the proliferation of social media.

On the one hand, social media makes it easier than ever for people to engage in discourse. People from all walks of life can sign up for a profile on Twitter, Facebook, Instagram, or any number of social media applications. Avatar in hand, they can instantly start engaging with people with completely different ideas, political beliefs, cultural upbringings, and even languages. I will grant you that the Internet at large was doing this long before social media came along, but social media continually makes it easier to converse with friends and strangers alike, all in real time.

As various platforms evolved, they also learned how to adapt to users' personal preferences. This meant that people could not only choose who to befriend or follow and what posts to like or dislike but also what kind of topics and stories they would like to see when they logged in. On the surface, curated timelines sound great: You get to see what you like and avoid what you dislike. However, when examined through the lens of public discourse and the exchange of conflicting ideas, this is one of the most blatant and pervasive forms of subconscious division.

We told the companies we wanted algorithms that locked us into tribes, we just didn't realize what that would mean. In short, we are trapped in bubbles of our own creation, but social media was the tool that helped us do it.

Like our ancient ancestors did, even in the virtual world we continue to form tribes. Perhaps you are really passionate about animal rights so you follow a page, group, or account dedicated to animal rights news. Thanks to the increasingly invasive algorithms of social media, apps like Facebook or Twitter can see what you like or what you engage with and present you with lists of other animal rights accounts or content. Over time, this pushes your brain into a bubble that only absorbs news or information that already aligns with your personal beliefs. Since you are rarely given the chance to see opposing viewpoints and are constantly barraged with opinions that mirror your own, you begin to feel that your view is patently right. Someone suggests that doing research on animals helps find cures for deadly diseases. You are more likely to treat them as wrong and, in many instances, react with condescension and hostility rather than engaging in civil discourse and listening to their ideas with an open mind. This often reinforces the position they already had. In a sense, the way you handle the conversation may be antithetical to your aims of bringing someone else on board or to at least have them understand your point of view. Hostility only makes someone more defensive of their own position.

It would be unfair to pin all the blame on social media giants. While they have perfected and actively profited off division and poor discourse, they did not invent the problem. Again, as humans, we are naturally inclined to gravitate toward like-minded people. We prefer to avoid conflict at the biological level—especially if we feel like there will be substantial repercussions or risks involved. But as we have all learned in recent years, people have a lot more confidence when they are hidden behind a keyboard (often earning some the title of "keyboard warriors" if they take particularly combative approaches online that they are unlikely to take in the physical world). This has made the online "troll" a nuisance and an active barrier to serious discourse. Unfortunately, with the rise of social media, trolls don't just live under the bridge anymore.

I do not mean to condemn the benefits of anonymity. In fact, being able to remain anonymous online also allows people to express themselves free of judgment or negative consequences. At *The Doe*, we appreciated giving people the security of anonymity in order to tell their stories and express themselves without fear of retribution. However, this same anonymity extends to many of our followers in the comment sections on social media. Civil discourse does take place, but many posts are infiltrated by trolls and bad-faith actors who simply want to rile people up and cause discord—knowing they will experience virtually no consequences. Our commitment to free speech and the aim of civil discourse means that we never remove comments unless they are actively causing harm to others and/or not adding to the discussion productively. Unfortunately, this still leaves plenty of room for people to practice poor discourse without triggering a response from our social media team.

After all, poor discourse is not something that can be measured or quantified. More importantly, it is not immutable. Poor discourse can be transformed into true civil discourse—if everyone is willing to engage sincerely. So avoiding poor discourse is not always about walking away from conversations or staying away from topics that could ignite fiery passion in yourself or others. Instead, it is about identifying the factors or people that are causing poor discourse and working to reframe the conversation in a more productive way.

The Double-Edged Sword of Social Media
QUESTIONS AND ANSWERS

Q: How can I know whether to walk away or try to improve the quality of the discourse?

A: There is no perfect answer to this question, but more often than not, it is better to stay and try to understand the other person's perspective, even when it feels unproductive. You should really only walk away from dialogue if you feel that there is absolutely no chance to engage in civil discourse or you believe that continuing could potentially cause harm to you or someone else. Feeling safe is important, and it is sometimes necessary to walk away when people disagree because there is always the chance that things could turn ugly. So you will need to evaluate discourse on a case-by-case basis, but try to avoid walking away unless you feel that it is absolutely necessary.

Q: Is it possible to overcome the intellectual "bubbles" that form on my social media?

A: Yes, but it takes some effort. Large social media companies know how to get you to click on articles that will make you angry or confirm your existing beliefs.

For these companies, it is all about getting the most clicks. This means that you should examine your timeline, knowing that it has been specifically curated by a constantly evolving algorithm to make you engage with posts, articles, and ads. This means that you should try to diversify the people in your social media circle. This way, you can prevent falling into an echo chamber and work against the algorithms that attempt to control your behavior.

IDENTIFYING BAD-FAITH ACTORS

Perhaps the number one cause of poor discourse is the involvement of bad-faith actors. These are people who have no intention of engaging in civil discourse; they simply want to disrupt, cause confusion, or incite anger in others. Excluding bad-faith actors and "trolls" may not always be easy or even possible. In these instances, you have few options beyond walking away. However, before you decide how to deal with these situations, you must first understand how to identify bad-faith actors both online and off.

Before we examine some real-world examples of bad-faith actors and evaluate the characteristics they share, it is important to note the difference between people who are *unconsciously* engaging in poor discourse and people who are actively *trying* to create poor discourse (i.e., bad-faith actors). The former group can simply be directed toward truth and mutually beneficial results (as we have discussed in previous chapters) while the latter group is far less likely to engage in anything honest, productive, or collaborative.

This distinction is vital because if you walk away from people who simply need help cultivating their ability to practice civil discourse, you risk creating even further division and taking an opportunity for open dialogue away from all parties involved.

One need only look to the January 6, 2021, storming of the US Capitol Building in Washington, DC. Thousands of then-president Donald Trump's supporters rioted and broke into the Capitol Building—an event that resulted in deaths, injuries, and dozens of arrests. When looking at the situation broadly, it was an outright attack on democracy and the legitimacy of our nation's electoral process. However, reporters covering the event took the time to interview individuals among the throngs of angry rioters only to discover that there was a wide array of positions, attitudes, and even emotions present.

Some rioters yelled expletives at the cameras and expressed outrage at the "stolen election." Others discussed their views more calmly and argued that they had every right to protest a government that, they believed, was not following the will of the people. Still others expressed concern over the growing chaos and mob mentality that was quickly taking shape, especially when some rioters began to break into the Capitol Building and clash with police officers.

Though there are many problems with the way in which news, information, and misinformation spread in the modern world, one beacon of hope lies in the sincerity of the journalistic process. Theoretically, journalists are meant to question and learn without taking sides or passing judgment. It goes without saying that many of today's "journalists" do not act in this way, but the palpable anger of the January 6 riots likely gave observers and journalists pause. They understood that something both momentous and dangerous was taking place. So rather than trying to incite more vitriol by asking loaded questions or antagonizing protesters, many of the on-the-ground journalists from media outlets like CNN and the Associated Press simply sought to understand the protestors, their message, and their endgame.

Despite the angry faces and violence, many protesters were willing to speak with media outlets to express their views clearly. They answered questions honestly and were forthright about what they believed. Even if some were misguided or basing their actions on conspiracy theories and tribalistic populism, they were still human beings with sincere convictions and a willingness to converse.

This goes to show that even in the most hostile environments, there is a place for civil discourse. Even when people are seemingly beyond reasoning, more than anything else, they want to be understood. This is one of the primary differences between people who are willing to engage in civil discourse and bad-faith actors. People who just want to "troll" often strive to push their own narrative, ignore direct lines of questioning, or use misdirection to deceive and confuse.

I am not saying that trolling lacks any place in discourse. Comedians often "troll" people to uncover funny or ironic truths about ourselves that have legitimate social value. Sacha Baron Cohen does this for a living. Despite sparking anger from many different groups, Cohen's characters, movies, and television programs have helped unearth the often unseemly views of others, all the while pretending to engage in real discourse. In his 2018 mockumentery series *Who Is America?*, Cohen convinced a conservative lawmaker from Georgia, Jason Spencer, to drop his pants and shout racial expletives on television, all in the name of fighting "Radical Islamism." Not only did this showcase the state representative's willingness to be overtly racist and xenophobic—in perhaps one of the most ridiculous circumstances possible—but it also brought a swift end to his political career.

However, outside of social satire, trolling tends to do far more harm than good. It makes it more difficult to differentiate truth from lies and honest participants from bad-faith actors. For this reason, it is important to identify characteristics of people who have no interest in civil discourse. Like discourse itself, identifying bad-faith actors requires practice. That said, research indicates[26] that people who engage in trolling or refuse to engage in true discourse share many of the same personality traits, including narcissism and a sense of pleasure in the misfortune of others. These people also often interact through manipulation and gaslighting.

For this reason, you must take the time to observe the behavior and mannerisms of others—especially if you suspect that they are actively trying to derail the discourse or manipulate you in some way. As I have discussed in previous chapters, you must always extend a certain degree of trust to others in order to practice civil discourse, but this does not mean you should take everything that they say at face value. There is still time for you to dig deeper into what they think, their motives, and what they are saying. Sometimes, it's more important to examine what they are *not* saying. Protecting yourself from bad-faith actors can ensure that you do not waste your time or become influenced by misinformation or outright lies.

Identifying Bad-Faith Actors
QUESTIONS AND ANSWERS

Q: Can civil discourse even happen with trolls and bad-faith actors?

A: The short answer is yes, but not easily. If someone decides to troll you or act in bad faith, you may have little recourse but to walk away. Holding up a mirror to someone who is being dishonest or trying to sow discord can work in some cases, but you should never underestimate the ability for some people to choose division over collaboration. So, if you feel that you are wasting your time with someone who refuses to engage with you sincerely, your efforts will be better spent elsewhere.

Q: Can people subconsciously act in bad faith?

A: Absolutely! This is why it is possible to help people understand how they are engaging in poor discourse or acting in bad faith. If someone is unaware of their behavior, you can act as an example of how true civil discourse works. With time, you can turn unintentional trolling into legitimate dialogue.

There's an approach we can take when people act in bad faith subconsciously, or if they act in ways that they seem less aware of. It's taking on the role of a light or torch. In a sense, you can politely and gently point someone toward a certain aspect of their behavior or thinking that's akin to acting in bad faith. This isn't guaranteed to work, but if you engage that person with the right openness and respect, you can help them see themselves in a new light, which can lead them to act in good faith.

ELEVATING THE CONVERSATION

F. Scott Fitzgerald might have put it best when he said, "To be kind is more important than to be right; many times, what people need is not a brilliant mind that speaks but a special heart that listens." It may sound overly sentimental, but it is the truth. More than anything else, civil discourse requires an open mind and an open heart. Being right may feel good for a brief moment, but being kind and open to others is far more productive in the long run.

Elevating the conversation is not just about taking the high road, showing respect to others, listening, and being attentive. It is also about moving the conversation into the real world. People often decry politicians and public figures for being "all talk and no action." Civil discourse has the power to break down the mental barriers that separate us, but without turning words into action, these words could fall into obscurity. Don't get me wrong; changing minds and learning through conversation is a productive activity on its own. On the global scale, greater discourse could help lead to solutions to many of the world's greatest crises—from global warming to income inequality.

That's the funny thing about discourse—it often leads to even more discourse. Having productive dialogues is like a snowball rolling down a mountain. As more people learn how to properly engage in civil discourse, it becomes easier to find the truth and reach mutually beneficial results. In other words, the snowball gets bigger and bigger until it is too big to stop. The key is to never lose faith in the process.

There is no doubt that we live in fractured times, and civil discourse feels like a pipe dream to some. But the reality is that civil discourse is attainable. All it takes is one conversation; one step in the right direction. With that, it means we are fixing one of the paramount issues of our time. If each of us takes it upon ourselves to have that one conversation and that one extra commitment to civil discourse, we can continue to make a difference. With time and practice, you will engage in discourse and improve your interactions each and every day—helping improve the world one conversation at a time.

Elevating the Conversation
QUESTIONS AND ANSWERS

Q: What if civil discourse does not lead to any kind of action? What if we just end up talking about it and moving on afterward?

A: There is nothing wrong with civil discourse that does not result in a specific action or solution. In the vast majority of cases, civil discourse simply results in the honest exchange of ideas. This may not lead to tangible results, but it does help move all participants closer to the truth (or mutually beneficial results). Elevating discourse to action does not always apply, and if you cannot collaboratively act on discourse, it does not mean that you have wasted your time. It only means that the discourse has allowed you and all other participants to learn from one another and reap the rewards of self-improvement.

RESETTING DETERIORATING DISCOURSE

There are times, however, when it no longer becomes possible to elevate discourse. Sometimes, emotions become too strained, and it is better to walk away from a discussion rather than let it deteriorate to incivility. There are instances when it is clear that bad-faith actors will not change their approach, and it is better to walk away than to waste time and frustration—especially because that frustration may boil over into your next conversation and lead to you having uncivil discourse even with a good-faith actor. In some cases, discourse simply deteriorates when strong personalities can't bear to compromise and frustration leads to incivility. Unfortunately, I watched this last scenario happen more than once within *The Doe*.

When I founded *The Doe*, I knew that I wanted to build a team of idealistic visionaries with a variety of perspectives across social, political, and other spectrums. Diversity of thought is essential in maintaining the integrity of any publication claiming to offer balanced perspectives. I recruited a team with varying backgrounds and worldviews, and we were always proud of the range of ideas that this brought to editorial, marketing, and even tech.

But as a team, our senior leadership struggled to find a clear product direction or to connect with our core population of readers. We couldn't come to agreements on revenue streams or fundraising timelines. Eventually, debates over how departments were understanding various terms deteriorated into battles over semantics. Team members reached ideological impasses.

Discourse often broke down between *The Doe*'s departments as senior leadership could not agree on shared priorities. A lack of central focus for product development meant opinions diverged and led to arguments over vision. Communication failed within departments as micromanaging displayed a lack of trust. As we discussed earlier, trust is such an essential part of ensuring civil discourse between people and within any community, so when trust breaks down within a company, so, too, does productive conversation.

Ultimately, broken discourse led to mistrust, and teams found it increasingly difficult to collaborate, which meant the company started to struggle. Product launches stalled, and marketing campaigns never materialized. It became necessary to restructure several teams and to make significant changes in leadership within multiple departments. It was frustrating to let go of talented individuals because we could not create a productive chemistry across the team. But there are times when it is necessary to reset deteriorating discourse for the good of the company as a whole.

My challenges with maintaining rapport at *The Doe* showed me that leading a company with a strong, social-good mission meant managing a team of highly passionate (at times overpowering) innovators. When you put that many artists and egos in the same room, you're bound to see disagreements turn into frustration and discourse fall into disarray. The best way to avoid having to reset deteriorating discourse within teams is to actively develop a culture of trust, reflection, listening, and attentiveness. It essentially means fostering open, productive, and civil discourse at every level of the organization.

Resetting Deteriorating Discourse
QUESTIONS AND ANSWERS

Q: What kind of fallout can there be if you reset deteriorating discourse?

A: All actions have consequences, and removing oneself or someone else from discourse can easily hurt people's feelings. Removing someone from a professional position and socially ostracizing others are extreme actions and should only be used if discourse has truly deteriorated. These are only measures you should take if it is impossible to get away from a bad-faith actor. Because these consequences can be severe, it really is better to try to avoid poor discourse in the first place. Working as hard as you can to bring positive, civil discourse to every conversation you enter is a great way to model positive discursive behavior and discourage deteriorating discourse.

SUMMARY

Poor discourse is common and can be difficult to avoid. However, *difficult* does not mean *impossible*. In the vast majority of cases, you can avoid poor discourse by getting out of your own intellectual "bubble" and engaging with others respectfully. You can even enhance poor discourse by identifying bad-faith actors and working to turn the conversation toward truth. Ultimately, you should aim to collaborate and use elevated civil discourse to find truth, mutually beneficial results, and workable solutions for real-world problems.

When attempting to enhance civil discourse or avoid poor discourse, just remember:

- If you only choose to engage with people who agree with you, you run the risk of turning yourself into a bad-faith actor. Try to reach out to those who have different ideas and opinions so that you can learn and grow.
- Don't be afraid to step away from dialogues that are unproductive. Unless you feel unsafe, do not run away just because a conversation is difficult. Instead, attempt to work past differences and find common ground.
- Pay attention to the behavior of others so that you can identify attempts to manipulate or spread misinformation.
- Sometimes it is necessary to reset discourse if it has become too uncivil, but the consequences are steep and you should always try to steer discourse back to civility when possible.
- Never lose faith in the process of civil discourse; even if you walk away feeling disheartened, remember that every conversation has something of value to offer.

FINAL QUESTIONS AND ANSWERS

Q: Avoiding poor discourse seems like a very important skill. How do I teach it to others?

A: Of course, the best way to teach those around you to avoid poor discourse is to always engage in good civil discourse yourself. Set an example of civil engagement in all your discussions with others. Try to utilize some of the ideas discussed in this chapter by sharing them. This is best done through discourse itself about these topics.

I wholeheartedly believe that it's a good idea to openly talk about the topic of avoiding poor discourse. Not everyone thinks about the difference between quality and poor discourse and may not have considered that it is more valuable to avoid poor discourse than to engage with ill intent. Encouraging others to consider reflection is a worthwhile effort. In particular, talking with kids about how to recognize and avoid poor discourse can help them minimize bullying in a way that does not further conflict. Similarly, I encourage all the leaders in my companies—and all companies—to recognize and avoid poor discourse within their departments to ensure harmonious and productive collaboration and brainstorming.

Q: I want to engage in civil discourse. What should I do next?

A: Get talking! Look for forums and outlets to discuss issues on your mind. Ask people questions. Start conversations. Remaining silent and failing to listen to others are the only ways to ensure that civil discourse cannot happen. So go out into the world with an open mind and a sincere conviction to learn and grow. Start practicing civil discourse as soon as possible!

Epilogue: Civil Discourse Going Forward

~

One important thing I've learned over the years is that the brokenness of how we get information is a multifaceted problem. It's a strange conundrum; we carry access to all the world's information, yet it feels as though we are more bombarded by lies than ever before.

We can consume any media we want—written, visual, and audial—with the swipe of a finger. It has all become easier and easier thanks to increasing Internet speed. But this reality has created challenges for news publications and other publishers. They were used to monopolizing media, be it through newspapers or news media outlets, but they needed to exist in the digital sphere. How could they make the move to the web and still be gatekeepers in a world that no longer had fences? The rules had changed. Anyone could publish on the web. The new world now meant that anyone could have a voice. Publishers went to social media, but they had a new problem—they had to compete with more things than ever online: brands you already like, your friends, and restaurants you already go to. They also didn't have to care about civil discourse—their focus was monetary. They used headlines that would generate the most clicks and interactions that would lead to subscriptions. They didn't care if they were divisive or not.

The problem was that publications would spew all this information through a biased lens. They weren't interested in solving civil discourse. In fact, the profit incentive actually led to the opposite. Many outlets stoked the fires of division and fear because that was a great way to trigger the more primal human drives for information.

So, as *The Doe* has evolved, I didn't want it to be some content mill that ended up being part of the problem. I brought in someone who knew how to build a publication—Josh Brandau, who was the chief revenue officer for the *Los Angeles Times* for three and a half years. He let me in on a little secret: massive publications are so huge and traditional that they aren't capable of solving modern problems. I made it my goal to solve those problems that the "old boys" could no longer handle.

Currently, I am working in tech and working with other publishers to create a real solution that brings publishing into the modern age of the web. That's why we pivoted to *Nota*, the next stage of evolution for *The Doe*. The goal with *Nota* is for writers to get paid for their work in real time through a royalty-based economic model. We will also ensure better verification and a better submission process for publishers.

Though I've come a long way from breeding turtles, I am still passionate about the ecosystem. Now, that ecosystem is one with greater content engagement—one that is balanced in all aspects, like the one where Sheldon and his family members thrived. I want *Nota* to be for publishing what Spotify is to music. *Nota* won't be like all the news sites that are bursting at the seams with ads. No matter how challenging, awkward, or stressful civil discourse may be, it is vital to our success as individuals, societies, and a species.

PRACTICING CIVIL DISCOURSE

Over the course of the preceding chapters, I laid out the factors that are most important in crafting civil discourse. I've suggested mindsets that you can utilize in your personal and professional life to become more comfortable with civil discourse and more capable of engaging in productive, meaningful conversations with others.

All civil discourse begins with trust and faith in the shared goal of mutually beneficial discussion. Gaining this trust in yourself and others requires reflection. That includes digging into your own biases, accepting your flaws, and working on undoing them. Reflection also helps us to understand our own intentions when engaging in discussion with others. While working to understand our own intent, we simultaneously work to identify bad intentions and push past the limits that ill-defined intent can place on discourse. Tone serves as the other foundation of civil discourse: the very expression of civility and respect in productive discourse comes from the use of a collaborative and inquisitive tone.

Civil discourse is more than just practicing good speech; it is about connecting with everyone involved in the discussion. Being an active listener who can maintain focus and show attentiveness will allow you to create a positive environment in which to practice civil discourse. Exercises that help us improve our listening skills and increase the time we can focus will be applicable for civil discourse at all levels of our lives, from the personal to the professional.

But as I've also discussed in this book, civil discourse is not easy; after all, if it were easy we would see far more of it today. We have to overcome the challenges that come from discussing contentious topics in an increasingly polarized world. That means actively building rapport to seek common ground and develop the kind of trust necessary to share opposing ideas respectfully. We have to expect that conflict will occur, but understand how to utilize that difference of opinion to reach an advanced understanding. Most of all, we have to be able to identify when poor discourse is occurring and locate the source of that uncivil behavior. Engaging in civil discourse means actively working to buck the trend toward hyperbole, and instead embrace discussion based on listening and respecting the self and others equally.

This book was a discourse with you as the reader and with society at large about the importance of civil discourse itself. Therefore, it does not come to a neat conclusion. Truly successful civil discourse doesn't need to come to a conclusion, and in fact may be just the beginning of a larger back-and-forth.

While we may come to conclusions as the product of the meaningful exchange of ideas, excellent civil discourse is about building a relationship that you can come back to and grow with. I think this is something that we forget today amidst the vitriol and polarization: civil discourse is about creating meaningful relationships as much as it is about sharing specific ideas. Excellent civil discourse builds bridges and opens opportunities for future discourse—future discussion of new, exciting, or even controversial ideas. We have truly succeeded in civil discourse when we have created a space for more discourse to occur, both for ourselves and for others.

AN AMERICAN LESSON ON RESTORING DISCOURSE

Thomas Jefferson's and John Adams's fifty-year friendship is one of the most powerful in American history. Their story provides a view of the impact of civil discourse, at levels both history changing and deeply personal. The two politicians met in 1775, and even though they were polar opposites physically, professionally, and ideologically, they formed a tight friendship built out of mutual respect for each other's intellect and passion.

Together, the two men led the rousing debates and discourse that would result in the Declaration of Independence and later the US Constitution. Both were skilled orators and writers, though Adams was known for yelling quite often. Through the strength of their discourse, the United States would become a free nation guided by well-reasoned rule of law and a symbol of discourse and democracy worldwide. Both men led at a time when civil discourse shaped the course of human politics in profound ways.

But even as close friends, these two ideologues often struggled to find common ground. During Adams's presidency, many historians note that discourse between Adams and his then-vice president Jefferson greatly declined, with vicious public arguments about the French Revolution. The 1800 presidential election set the two against each other again, and with Jefferson's victory, the two began a twelve-year period where they refused to speak to each other.

It would in fact be civil discourse that would bring the two legends back together. Mutual friend Benjamin Rush corresponded with each Founding Father and wrote of a dream he'd had that the two reconnected through letter writing. Adams and Jefferson took the hint and rekindled their friendship through spirited discourse in the form of letters. Historians today can pour through the surviving 185 letters that Jefferson and Adams sent to each other for the last fourteen years of their lives. Their words display a deepening friendship built on respect and even tenderness, expressed through brilliant civil discourse.

Both men passed away on the exact same day within a few hours of each other. One might suspect that if there is some form of afterlife, the two men headed off together to continue their passionate and fiery debates. But in a wonderful historical coincidence, that day when both Thomas Jefferson and John Adams died was July 4, 1826: the fiftieth anniversary of the day the Declaration of Independence was announced. As they took their last breaths, fellow Americans were unknowingly cheering in the streets, celebrating the consequences of the discourse they had led fifty years before.

Their story is a perfect example of how civil discourse can change our lives at the societal level and the personal level. But the story of Thomas Jefferson and John Adams also warns us that even the most brilliant people can fall into uncivil discourse and can struggle to maintain civility and respectfulness. Their relationship then reminds us that struggles with civil discourse can be overcome, setbacks can be righted, and broken relationships mended. Maintaining, encouraging, and engaging in civil discourse is a lifelong effort requiring growth and practice. There are always new opportunities for improvement but also great discursive moments we can celebrate as we achieve them.

TAKING LESSONS FORWARD

Writing this book has been a part of my journey toward fostering civil discourse, but it's a part of a larger picture. We each must work actively and with intention to be better listeners and more respectful speakers, and to promote these values personally and professionally. We should approach practicing civil discourse as a lifelong pursuit, just as we should try to maintain good eating and exercise habits. With that goal in mind, this book has provided suggestions for making civil discourse a part of your daily life.

But what can we do going forward, individually and collectively, to foster more civil discourse within our society or in digital environments? Of course, we won't all build companies and try to disrupt industries. But there are many ways that you can engage in promoting civil discourse in your community:

- Serve as a role model within your professional environment. Engage in civil discourse at company meetings. Be attentive to your coworkers and listen to their insights. Additionally, encourage those with differing perspectives to find common ground.

- Get involved in organizations in your community where you can model civil discourse. Run for local office, join the PTA, or take a leadership position in your religious organization. In whatever you choose, you will promote civil discourse by modeling it and practicing it in your own leadership.

- Support programs and activities that teach civil discourse skills to the next generation. That includes encouraging kids to work on meditation and self-reflection. They can also take part in activities that promote good listening skills and collaborating toward common goals. Uplift coaches and program directors who promote civil discourse within their programming.

- While we all don't want to become entrepreneurs building companies to promote civil discourse, if you have a brilliant idea, please build it. Don't be afraid that the task is too daunting, and don't run away from one of the greatest challenges of our generation. Some of the most successful companies and some of the most monumental technological advances have been born in the garages of big-dreaming innovators; so, too, will it be for discourse. Improving civil discourse will take many approaches simultaneously, so turn your dreams into reality and become a part of the solution.

Moving to a more individual level, everyone is able to improve the quality of the discourse in their personal lives. This means not only utilizing the lessons learned from this text but sharing those lessons with others. If we want a wider discussion about the art of civil discourse, then we all have to go out and bring others into that debate, starting with our closest discussants—family, friends, coworkers, and colleagues. There are many ways we can take the lessons of this book and affect them in our personal lives:

- **Embrace self-reflection, meditation, concentration, and personal growth.** Civil discourse begins with participants who are in the right frame of mind to uplift one another's ideas, and that begins with your own mindset and approach.
- **Explore books, apps, and activities, which help you improve your listening, attention, and focus skills.** This will not only improve your civil discourse but also improve your ability to identify and walk away from ill-intentioned or poor discourse.
- **Start discussions.** The only way you can truly practice civil discourse is by engaging in it, and sometimes that means taking the risk and starting the conversation yourself. Join

discursive communities, both in real life and online, and practice civil discourse with others. Even if it feels uncomfortable at first, you will get better over time with practice!

SUMMARY

All this is to say that the art of civil discourse is like any other art: it must be practiced continuously and shared openly with others. Historical precedents—like in the case of Jefferson and Adams—tell us that civil discourse and conversation is necessary, even when it is hard and even when it feels impossible. Part of the reason that reflection, meditation, focus, and active listening are so essential to civil discourse is that practicing it can be exhausting, frustrating, and challenging. It's an art, and like a ballerina who practices their choreography and forms a thousand times before each performance, you must practice civil discourse as much as possible. You must hone the skills you'll need at the most important discursive moments in your life.

Civil discourse has the power to change the world for good on the societal level and also at the deeply personal level. The examples in this book have demonstrated this, and I am hopeful that the techniques and practices described here will allow you to engage in meaningful, productive civil discourse going forward. The first step of improving your discourse is reflection, so let this closing of this book begin that process for you!

FINAL THOUGHTS

You can't change everyone's mind. You can't always find common ground. Maybe you're planning to throw this book in the trash when you're done because that's where you think my opinions belong. You know what, that's okay. I tried.

There's a natural propensity in many of us to want to validate feeling right, but none of us are perfect. I know I'm still learning as I go, and I've come to realize that the only constant we have is change. We need to be able to swim along with the flow of new information, and give people the space to speak their minds. It is crucial that we discuss with civility, care, and respect.

I'm just saying—I was once (and maybe sometimes still am) the kid with terrible discourse. I'd get in arguments on social media and in person. I'd glare from atop the pedestal I'd built for myself and talk down to anyone with a differing opinion. But I learned a valuable lesson—being combative will never build discourse; it will only break discourse.

To have the best possible conversation—one that's open, successful, and deepens our connection to other humans—look at each discussion as a gateway to a solution, not just a way to vent your opinion and create more problems. Most of us place ourselves into tribes and surround ourselves with like-minded people. Unfortunately, all this does is reinforce the echo chamber. It makes civil discourse too difficult when any dissenting voice is drowned out.

So, I'm just saying—if there's anything I want you to take away from this book, it's this:

Have conversations with people you disagree with. Be open to their perspectives and try to find why they've come to a different conclusion. Understand where they're coming from, and always see them in their humanness. Remember that they have flaws, are vulnerable, and crave connection—just like you.

That's how we're going to move on. That's how we'll heal our world.

I'm just saying.

Endnotes and Recommended Readings

~

ENDNOTES

1. Katie Couric, interview with Justin Baldoni, *Next Question with Katie Couric,* podcast audio, (July 21, 2021), https://katiecouric.com/podcast/next-question/justin-baldoni-man-enough-book-kids-wife/

2. William Hart, *The Art of Living: Vipassana Meditation: As Taught by S. N. Goenka* (New York: Harper Collins, 1987).

3. Sarah Wilson, "Paul Ekman, the Master of Micro-Expressions," *The Guardian* (Guardian News and Media, March 7, 2009), https://www.theguardian.com/lifeandstyle/2009/mar/07/micro-facial-expressions-poker-face

4. Paul Ekman, *Telling Lies: Clues to Deceit in the Marketplace, Politics, and Marriage* (New York: W. W. Norton & Company, 2009), 149.

5. Alexandra Hutzler, "Maddow Calling Oan 'Russian Propaganda' Protected by First Amendment: Court," *Newsweek* (Newsweek, August 17, 2021), https://www.newsweek.com/court-rules-rachel-maddow-calling-oan-russian-propaganda-protected-first-amendment-1620338

6. David Moye, "Tucker Carlson Admits He Sometimes Lies on His Show," *Huff-Post* (HuffPost, September 14, 2021), https://www.huffpost.com/entry/tucker-carlson-admits-lying-on-show_n_613fb9bee4b09519c5085ebd

7. Joe Biden, "Remarks by President Biden After Meeting with Members of the COVID-19 Response Team" (Press Briefing, Washington DC, December 16, 2021), The White House, https://www.whitehouse.gov/briefing-room/speeches-remarks/2021/12/16/remarks-by-president-biden-after-meeting-with-members-of-the-covid-19-response-team/

8. Oprah Winfrey, "Commencement Speech, 2019, Colorado College" (Commencement Speech, Colorado Springs, CO, May 19, 2019), Colorado College, https://www.youtube.com/watch?v=iZ5-tmzhfFU&ab_channel=BloombergQuicktake%3ANow

9. Asurion, "Americans Check Their Phones 96 Times a Day," (Press Release, Asurion, November 21, 2019), https://www.asurion.com/press-releases/americans-check-their-phones-96-times-a-day/

10. Stephen King, *On Writing: A Memoir of the Craft* (New York, Scribner, 2010), 17.

11. "Ford's Five-Dollar Day," The Henry Ford Org (Henry Ford Org, January 3, 2014), https://www.thehenryford.org/explore/blog/fords-five-dollar-day/

12. Renée Peltz Dennison, "Do Half of All Marriages Really End in Divorce?" *Psychology Today* (Sussex Publishers, April 24, 2017), https://www.psychologytoday.com/us/blog/heart-the-matter/201704/do-half-all-marriages-really-end-in-divorce

13. Julie Tseng and Jordan Poppenk, "Brain meta-state transitions demarcate thoughts across task contexts exposing the mental noise of trait neuroticism," *Nature Communications* 11, no. 3480 (July 2020). https://doi.org/10.1038/s41467-020-17255-9

14. Chella Man, "Becoming Him" (Ted Talk, Tinton Falls, NJ, April 7, 2018), Ranney School, https://www.ted.com/talks/chella_man_becoming_him

15. Andrew Wilkinson, Twitter Post, Feb 28, 2022, 9:07 AM, https://twitter.com/awilkinson/status/1498298758089490433

16. Norah O'Donnell, "Bridging America's political divide with conversations, "One Small Step" at a time," *60 Minutes* (CBS News, January 9, 2022), https://www.cbsnews.com/news/one-small-step-storycorps-60-minutes-2022-01-10/

17. Milan Kordestani, "Putting the United Back in the United States: An Open Letter to My Political Counterpart," *HuffPost* (BuzzFeed, July 3, 2017), https://www.huffpost.com/entry/putting-the-united-back-in-the-united-states-an-open_b_5959c5a7e4b0f078efd98b3d

18. Sanghoon Kang and Terri R. Kurtzberg, "Reach for your cell phone at your own risk: The cognitive costs of media choice for breaks," *Journal of Behavioral Addictions* 8, no 3 (Sept 2019): 395–403. https://doi.org/10.1556/2006.8.2019.21

19. Shunryu Suzuki, *Zen Mind, Beginner's Mind: Informal Talks on Zen Meditation and Practice* (Boulder, Shambhala Publications, 2011).

20. Matt Ornstein, dir., *Accidental Courtesy: Daryl Davis, Race & America* (Sound & Vision Productions, 2017), Prime Video.

21. Ornstein, 2017

22. Max Amini, "Max Amini - "Dodool Tala" ...... Please Share :)", YouTube, July 1, 2013, https://www.youtube.com/watch?app=desktop&v=lQmJlw483eE

23. Pascal Wallisch, "Two Years Later, We Finally Know Why People Saw "The Dress" Differently," *Slate* (Slate Group, April 12, 2017), https://slate.com/technology/2017/04/heres-why-people-saw-the-dress-differently.html

24. Wallisch, 2017

25. Christopher Ojeda and Peter K. Hatemi, "Accounting for the Child in the Transmission of Party Identification," *American Sociological Review* 80, no 6 (2015): 1150. https://doi.org/10.1177/0003122415606101

26. Erin E.Buckels, Paul D.Trapnell, and Delroy L.Paulhus, "Trolls just want to have fun," *Personality and Individual Differences* 67, (Sept 2014): 97-102. https://doi.org/10.1016/j.paid.2014.01.016

RECOMMENDED READINGS

• Aurelius, Marcus. *Meditations*. Translated by Martin Hammond. New York: Penguin Classics, 2006.

• Covey, Stephen M. R., and Rebecca R. Merrill. *The Speed of Trust: The One Thing That Changes Everything*. New York: Free Press, 2018.

• Epictetus. *The Discourses of Epictetus: Epictetus*. Translated by George Long. Amazon: Createspace Independent Publishing Platform, 2016.

• Patterson, Kerry, Joseph Grenny, Ron McMillan, and Al Switzler. *Crucial Conversations: Tools for Talking When Stakes Are High*. New York: Mcgraw-Hill Professional, 2012.

• Stone, Douglas, Bruce Patton, and Sheila Heen. *Difficult Conversations: How to Discuss What Matters Most*. New York: Penguin Books, 1999.

Acknowledgments

Writing about civil discourse was first and foremost a conversation with myself. I cherish the moments, alone with my laptop, when I can work through a topic that I am deeply motivated to explore through research and my own words. Writing this book was an opportunity to reflect and uncover valuable insights from my life that can help others who, like me, have learned to question—and respectfully discuss—the most uncomfortable of topics.

As this book becomes part of a greater conversation, it's my privilege to thank those who supported me in this journey. This is my first book, originally envisioned by Monica Meehan and Michelle Meade, who found my work, believed in the need for a book on civil discourse, and drove me to create my first proposal.

I want to thank my literary agents, Leticia Gomez and Raoul Davis, for helping me find a publisher that understood the complexity of this topic. I am extremely grateful for my publisher, Health Communications, Inc., for taking a chance on me, and offering support and guidance every step of the way. In particular, I want to thank my editor, Christine Belleris, for helping me develop the book into something that would be relatable and useful for many. The tone and narrative also benefited greatly from the insights of Seth Miller, Nathan Hassall, and Matthew Jones.

I want to thank my advisors, M. Chloe Mulderig, Samuel Evans, and Cleo Stiller, for their guidance and support. Thank you to all the team members who helped make The Doe a reality and believed in our mission.

My most heartfelt appreciation is for my mom, dad, and sister, Misha, for always supporting me and keeping me grounded in my pursuit to make a positive impact on the world. I am also grateful to my friends, family members, and all the individuals whose voices and stories I analyzed in this work.

Writing this book was a challenging yet fulfilling and enlightening journey, with more individuals who inspired me throughout this process than I can thank on this page. Nonetheless, I am grateful for the support and contributions of all those who inspired moments of pause and reflection for me to compile this guide. With time, I hope this book can inspire others to engage in civil discourse, propelling common-ground solutions for a rapidly changing society.

About the Author

~

Milan Kordestani is a social entrepreneur and author who advocates for common-ground solutions to systemic socioeconomic problems. Kordestani's environmental studies background allowed him to understand humanity's impact on earth systems and to see why societal attempts to mitigate the environmental crisis have failed. As a result, he shifted his focus to founding numerous businesses– *Nota*, Audo, and Guin–each of which offers a sustainable solution for a core systemic issue across civil discourse, education, and culture. Through his businesses and writing, Kordestani encourages the next generation to find solutions that drive positive societal change. He has published his perspectives on topics like civil discourse, the future of work, conscious capitalism, and the publishing industry regularly in outlets such as *HuffPost, Entrepreneur,* and *Rolling Stone.*